Paddy Moloney

Paddy Moloney and the Chieftains

BILL MEEK

SIDGWICK & JACKSON
LONDON

First published in Great Britain in 1987 by
Sidgwick & Jackson Limited
Originally published in Ireland by
Gill and Macmillan Ltd
Copyright © 1987 by Paddy Moloney

ISBN 0-283-99554-8
Designed by Jarlath Hayes
Printed in Hong Kong for Sidgwick & Jackson Limited
1 Tavistock Chambers
Bloomsbury Way
London WCIA 2SG

The publishers have made every effort to trace
copyright holders of the photos reproduced. If any
source has been overlooked, the publishers will be
happy to make the appropriate arrangements.

Author's acknowledgments

I would like to thank my wife, Pauline, for the
care with which she read the original script
and for her sometimes devastating but always
constructive comments. I would also thank Rita
Moloney for gallons of China tea consumed during
my sessions with Paddy.

Contents

1 *Introduction*

Not many years after the end of the second world war, a young piper in short trousers played his first public concert. The venue was a draughty hall situated in a decaying square on the north side of the city of Dublin. The musician was Paddy Moloney.

A few miles west of that spot the same piper, now three decades older, was to lead the group he founded to play before an audience well in excess of a million souls. This time the venue was the Phoenix Park and the event, the visit of a Pope.

These two occasions somehow epitomise the remarkable story of Paddy Moloney and the Chieftains. It is a story with a worldwide scenario, yet rooted in the musical traditions of a rather small island lying to the west of the continent of Europe. Why is it that a band specialising in a non-commercial form of ethnic music has built a massive following so far and wide? The music itself provides a large part of the answer, and Paddy has often voiced his basic conviction: *'We let the music speak for itself.'*

It is of course a music full of heart, developed over the centuries by people of little or no property, compelling, lively, and tearful. Through the combination of luck, hard work, but mostly honest musicianship it has been the lot of the Chieftains to spread its sound and spirit to people far removed from the culture where it originated, giving them, as Susannah York put it, 'memories I've never had'.

And yet this tale is hardly typical of most success stories emerging from the world of entertainment during the second half of the twentieth century. Where are the gimmicks? A writer once likened the visual image of the Chieftains on stage to a cluster of civil servants. What he meant was that they are almost unique in being so unconventional as to garb themselves conventionally. Gimmicks such as outlandish 'gear', startling props, or puffs of smoke play no part in the act. *The music speaks for itself.*

How can the continuity of their popularity be explained? A year or two of successful touring is not an uncommon achievement for the more notable folk groups. But the Chieftains will celebrate their quarter century in 1988. Every year has seen their following increase, and every year has brought its fresh crop of 'firsts' — first Irish folk ensemble to be named *Melody Maker* 'group of the year', first band to play in the Capitol building of the United States, first musicians in history to perform on the Great Wall of China, first Irish group to win an Oscar. The answer must be that the Chieftains not only continually conquer new audiences but also retain the love and affection of former conquests.

Perhaps the most astonishing fact is that in the beginning the band really got together for a 'once-off' operation. Although Paddy and his original colleagues were accustomed to playing in each other's company and had confidence in each other's abilities, it is also true that the collective term 'The Chieftains' was first used in 1963 by five musicians who had gathered to prepare a programme of music with the singular purpose of cutting one LP. Four of them lived in Dublin: Paddy worked for a builders' supplier, Martin Fay was a purchasing agent, Michael Tubridy a consulting engineer, and Seán Potts an official in the Department of Posts and Telegraphs. The fifth member, the late Davey Fallon, travelled up from County Westmeath to take part in those preparatory sessions. At the time it could scarcely have struck any of them that this was but the first of many albums, or that the seeds were being sown for a full-time commitment to music.

In the ensuing years, as might be expected, there have been personnel changes. In 1966 Davey Fallon was replaced on bodhrán by Peadar Mercier who was in turn succeeded by Kevin Conneff. Seán Keane joined Martin Fay in the fiddle section, and in the early seventies Derek Bell augmented the original sound with his harp. In time Seán Potts decided to forgo a travelling life-style and Mick Tubridy handed over the flute spot to Matt Molloy in 1979.

All past and present members have left their mark on the style of the group, and despite the changes there has been a continuity of spirit. One essential element in this has been the continuous function of Paddy as musical director as well as founder of the Chieftains. Why Paddy? There are many answers to that but perhaps the most pertinent one was offered by Martin a number of years ago: 'Because we want it that way'. So it is appropriate that the telling of this story should be as seen through the eyes of Paddy.

In the course of their long career, the Chieftains have involved themselves in a wide range of musical experiences. They have appeared before vast audiences on the broadcasting media, have played with chamber, concert, and symphony orchestras, have been associated with rock groups, have performed with folk musicians from diverse cultures, have provided music for ballet, legitimate theatre, pantomime, and the cinema with Paddy becoming an accomplished arranger and composer of film scores. Yet there is a definite line of continuity running through their work from the earliest days to the present time. Although their musical scope may cover a broad spectrum, they have none the less never lost the initial devotion to traditional music. This fact is a vital element in the secret of their success.

Another is the manner in which audiences react to them on stage. This is something which cannot really be described in words; it has to be experienced through witnessing what goes on between musicians and listeners during a live performance. Laughter has something to do with it, for laughter is never far below the surface. Above all the Chieftains never fail to pass on to the audience just how much they enjoy playing their music. This sets in motion a sort of chain reaction which touches all present and gladdens their hearts. It is small wonder that Paddy places the highest priority on live tours, even if each individual concert is viewed by only a tiny fraction of those who might tune in to a major television show.

Maintaining a sense of humour off as well as on-stage is another ingredient to the successful survival of the group. Paddy has an ability to respond with humour to all sorts of situations. Typical of this was the occasion when he was awakened by a telephone at the crack of dawn in a Canadian hotel. On the line was a journalist in a state of excitement to pass on the news that a visiting British 'royal' had been reported as referring to the Irish as 'pigs'. After an initial outburst of expletives, Paddy composed himself. 'I tell you what,' said he, 'by our next concert we'll have a piece of music in her honour.' The result was 'If I had Maggie in the Wood'. The words to this opus go as follows:

> If I had Maggie in the wood
> I'd do her all the good I could,
> If I had Maggie in the wood
> I'd keep her there till morning.

As far back as January 1976, the Chieftains found themselves featured in the lead music column of *Time* magazine. According to *Time:*

> They are, in short, about as average a bunch as any country can produce and not the usual candidates for pop stardom. But when they sit down together to play, they are something else again: the Chieftains, Ireland's leading folk band. Their music is climbing the pop charts of England — not because they are Irish but because they sing no songs and instead spin out purified instrumentals of the reel, jig, slide, Kerry polka and other such traditional forms. On their last two visits to London they packed Albert Hall. Midway through a three-week American tour in November, they sold out Avery Fisher Hall at New York City's Lincoln Center, where young Irish Americans danced jubilantly in the aisles. Last week they were back in Manhattan to highlight an all-Irish programme at Carnegie Hall.

This particular sample of international media exposure dates back to a time when the band had been in operation as a full-time professional group for only a few months. It is a prime example of the way the media have always been attracted to the group. Part of the explanation is that journalists probably feel a natural affinity for a crowd of musicians who seem oblivious to the superficial trappings of fame so carefully nurtured by so many aspirants to stardom. But be it admitted, it is also the result of carefully planned campaigns on the part of Paddy and the expert publicists to whom he has entrusted the image of the band.

The emphasis on instrumental music mentioned by the writer in *Time* is in itself a unique aspect of the Chieftains' achievement. When they first began to catch the attention of the public in the 1960s, there was an international interest in folk-oriented music, but generally this centred on singing groups or individual singers. Quite a number of Irish artists were to attract a following in different parts of the world, but their concentration was on songs with the instrumentals as a secondary feature. The Chieftains blazed a different sort of trail by reversing this procedure: their mission was to spread the sound of the instrumental tradition. In doing so they opened up new geographic territory which benefited other Irish musicians following many different musical trends.

As the band began to concentrate increasingly on foreign tours, its members might well have found themselves growing further and further away from the root source of their music. Happily this has not happened. Each Chieftain is in his own right an accomplished solo player enjoying the company of other musicians. When they are not touring it is quite common for them as individuals to get together for sessions with home-based instrumentalists in their own community circles. This means they are constantly in touch with the traditional scene in Ireland, and that there is little danger of the members of the band ever being allowed to remove themselves from their musical roots.

This association with living Irish music is fortified by a continued commitment to Irish audiences. Successful appearances in far-flung places such as New York, Melbourne, or Shanghai have not diminished the importance that Paddy would place on proving equally successful in Dublin, Belfast, or for that matter the smallest village in rural Ireland. But it is also true that even within Ireland their attraction reaches out to people who are otherwise not especially involved in traditional music.

Of course the world is small, especially for the Chieftains. An example of just how small arose after a concert in Hong Kong in 1983. Paddy found himself being addressed by a member of the audience:

'Do you not recognise me?'

The voice was Irish but the face failed to register.

'I'm the fellow who pulled you out of the ditch when your car got stuck up the Sally Gap last summer.'

The man was right. It had been the culmination of a long story, but he had in fact pulled Paddy's car out of a ditch on a lonely mountain road in the early hours of a morning that previous summer.

What follows is the story of the Chieftains to date. The band itself was formed some twenty-three years ago, but the origins of the saga stretch back to the forties. It is of course an unfinished story. In the sphere of professional music only a fool would dare to predict the future. This writer is prepared to take the risk. All the indications suggest that in the years to come there will be many more instalments to the tale of Paddy Moloney and the Chieftains.

Paddy Moloney, musical director and founder of the Chieftains, was born in the year 1938. Home was in Donnycarney on the north side of the city of Dublin. It was an area where a number of well-known musicians happened to live, so there was music in the air. There was also music in the house, for both Paddy's parents inherited the tradition from their native county of Laois. His grandfather was an accomplished flute player and an uncle an enthusiastic member of the Ballyfin Pipe Band.

As well as music in the house there was also dancing. Paddy recalls that on Sunday evenings in particular cousins, uncles, and aunts together with the odd neighbour would call in to sing and dance the night away. The table would be pulled back for the

13

The group in 1975 – a promotional picture taken for Island Records

14

half-sets to begin. If there wasn't a live instrument to hand, his job, although not yet five years old, was to re-load the needles on the old HMV gramophone.

Around that time, his own musical career began. His first instrument was a whistle, not actually a tin whistle but a plastic model with a red top which his mother bought at Bolgers of North Earl Street on Christmas Eve for the sum of one shilling and nine pence. This he taught himself to play at the age of six.

School for Paddy was Scoil Mhuire, run by the Christian Brothers in the nearby district of Marino. Here the musical environment complemented the atmosphere at home and he still regards his teachers with affection and gratitude. One in particular, a Brother McCaffrey, was keen on traditional music and taught him tonic solfa. Having mastered this, he was able to pick up tunes quickly and even jot them down as he heard them played.

Once the dreaded visit of an inspector turned to a moment of triumph.

'Moloney!'

'Yes, Sir.'

'Think of a tune.'

'"The Blackbird".'

'Right. I'd like you to sing it in tonic solfa.'

The old band in 1975 in happy form after signing with Island Records

15

This he proceeded to do to perfection, to the delight of the inspector and teacher — as well as his own relief.

In time his instrumental experience widened. For a while he took piano lessons and also amused himself with a ukelele. However gradually he came to the realisation that his abiding musical love was going to be the uilleann pipes. One of the teachers, a fiddler by the name of Brother Forrestal, ran a school band which included a set of pipes played by a fellow-pupil called Leon Rowsome. Paddy decided that this was the instrument for him and ran home to tell his mother in a state of childish excitement.

Astute woman that she was, his mother took this enthusiasm sufficiently seriously to approach Leo Rowsome, 'The King of the Pipers' and the father of the young musician who had so impressed her son. Leo, who was a nationally-known musician, teacher, and pipe-maker, informed her that a practice set suitable for a young learner would cost in the region of £5. It was an enormous sum of money to try and find. Paddy's father was in the Irish army and at the time this amounted to something like a week's wages. Yet through saving and sacrifice the cash was put together, the pipes purchased, and Paddy enrolled for weekly lessons with Leo at the School of Music in Chatham Street.

The lessons proved popular with the boy for reasons apart from the furthering of musical ambitions. The school was close-by the Gaiety Theatre, and he would sometimes persuade his mother to bring him there afterwards, especially if Jimmy O'Dea, the famous Dublin comedian, was on the bill. At that time it cost a shilling for the balcony, but often he dashed ahead to settle himself in a seat before his mother had got so far as the ticket-box, where the lady had the kind habit of pretending that she hadn't seen him.

Leo Rowsome died a number of years ago, but Paddy still regards him with enormous respect both as a teacher and a musician. He used to listen spellbound to the recitals he gave both on radio and at the Pipers' Club, and was especially pleased that Claddagh should have featured him on their very first album, whilst still maintaining that no recording ever fully captured the real genius of the artist.

Paddy vividly remembers his first public concert at Ozanam House in Mountjoy Square, at a function organised by St Vincent de Paul. With about seven other pipers, all of them older and taller, he played his way through 'Saddle the Pony' and 'Donnybrook Fair' with Leo vamping the chords on a piano. It was 'a great and wonderful occasion'.

Competitions were all the rage at the time and at ten years of age after twelve months' tuition he was entered as the youngest competitor in the under-fourteen piping section of the Feis Átha Cliath in the Mansion House. Being judged fourth proved a great disappointment. The following year however he took first place amid scenes of jubilation. There had been over twenty competitors and all of them older than he. As Leo carried him down the hall on his shoulders, he heard an old man remark, 'That fellow must have been here before.' Unknown to himself, one of those who witnessed all of this was his future friend and fellow-Chieftain Seán Potts.

The founding of Comhaltas Ceoltóirí Éireann in 1951 led to the institutionalising of

On top of the world – or rather on top of Tommy Hamill's scrapyard wall at Milltown

competitive playing on a national scale. Paddy was to win all-Ireland medals on three occasions, but on reaching the venerable age of sixteen decided to put competitions behind him. Already he had strong reservations about competitive playing, as he does to this day.

In the summertime he would spend holidays, remembered as golden times of unbroken joy, at his grandparents' place in Sconce, in the foothills of the Slieve Bloom mountains near the village of Ballyfin in County Laois. It is an area noted for its wealth in tradition, legend, and lore with the music a part of all of that.

His mother had told him stories of the past, such as tales of the crossroad dances when the crowds gathered on *fraochán* (bilberry) Sunday. The picking of the fruit was followed by 'music till morning', with women in long dresses dancing to the light of flickering bonfires. His grandfather was one of the musicians, and Paddy remembers him as a flute player of great taste. Often he would bring him 'rambling', sometimes to visit another flute player who used to keep his instrument under a stone in the river.

Mid 1970s at Thomas Street in Dublin

'He reckoned this the best place to store it in the interests of security, and because he believed the moist atmosphere preserved its tone.'

Most Saturday nights there was dancing from about eight in the evening until time for mass in the morning. The sets were accompanied mostly by fiddles and melodeons, with the boy joining in using two spoons on a tin pail, and in later times the whistle. About three hours into the night, a huge kettle was boiled to wet the tea for the first sitting of supper, and then the songs would start. Thereafter more dancing, lively and relaxed — full-sets, half-sets, and polkas.

The summer when he brought his practice set of uilleann pipes to Laois it caused great excitement as the instrument was a novelty in that part of the country. His uncle of course played the highland pipes and used to bring Paddy as a mascot when the Ballyfin band marched up and down the streets of nearby towns such as Birr and Roscrea to gather funds. He was placed on the bass drum to play his own practice set as the people threw in their donations. But at the age of fourteen he acquired his first

Seán Potts and Paddy Moloney playing a duet at the twenty-first birthday concert at the National Concert Hall, Dublin

19

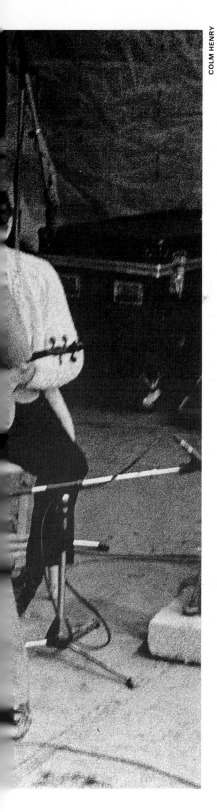

Peadar Mercier with Pat Kilduff, the lilter, who appeared on The Chieftains 3 *album, at a concert in 1972 at the National Stadium, Dublin*

In the window of the late-lamented Royal Hibernian Hotel, Dublin

Paddy and Derek in one of their humorous exchanges

21

full set of uilleann pipes, to add the challenge of drones and regulators to that of chanter and bag.

During those early formative years Paddy was already developing his individual approach to the instrument, resorting to both the supposedly opposed 'open' and 'tight' fingering styles to meet the demands of different tunes. To develop his own technique was a necessity as well as being his inclination, for when he took lessons with Leo there simply wasn't time to cover such aspects; and outside of formal tuition, the piping fraternity was not renowned for sharing the mysteries of the art. And yet this

The Chieftains past and present when they were awarded the first-ever platinum disc by IFPI for sales in excess of quarter of a million, presented to them on the Late Late Show

development of style was totally unconscious, for he himself was never aware that the process was in operation.

Luckily, opportunities arose to listen to the great exponents, to men such as Jimmy Ennis, known for his beautiful musical embellishments and the father of the late Seamus Ennis, himself a splendid piper and one of the great collectors of all time. As luck would have it, in Donnycarney there were two other well-known piping households close to the Moloney home, in addition to the Rowsome residence. Dan Dowd, a piper who has worked all his life to promote every aspect of the art, lived nearby. So too did Peter Flynn, whose dedication to the instrument had been physically inhibited by the loss of a finger during the War of Independence, in which he had served as an officer in the volunteers. His most prized possession was a chanter which had belonged to Eamonn Ceannt, one of the executed signatories to the 1916 proclamation. Of all his piping guests, Paddy alone was privileged to finger his historic relic. But apart from the music, Paddy's abiding memory is of Maggie Flynn's home-made bread and jam.

Most Monday nights Flynn's home was open house to musicians, and those attending included some of the foremost pipers in the land. There was Jack Wade, Mícheál Ó Riabhaigh, Seamus Ennis, Sean Reid, and Tommy Reck. The late Breandán Breathnach, who eventually founded Na Píobairí Uilleann (The Association of Uilleann Pipers), used to come along to play as did the man from Clare, Willie Clancy. Willie, already a veteran on the tin whistle, was just commencing a brilliant piping career which he pursued up to the time of his early death.

Although still in his teens, nothing pleased Paddy more than to take part in lively sessions at venues such as the Pipers' Club in Thomas Street, or the rival establishment across the river Liffey in Church Street. As well as Dublin musicians, these might be attended by instrumentalists from out of town such as the Doran brothers, pipers of the travelling tradition, whom he remembers well. Once Felix Doran handed Paddy his pipes: the experience 'nearly destroyed' him. Felix was a huge man and the pipes full of leaks which didn't bother him, but as Paddy recollects, 'They nearly killed me trying to keep the wind in them.'

Sometimes the literary and the traditional worlds got together and Paddy remembers playing the whistle to accompany Brendan Behan, a regular visitor to the Pipers' Club, as the writer sang the 'Druimfhionn Donn Dilis', one of the big songs in the Gaelic tradition. 'He actually could hit high F, even if he was red in the gills with the effort.'

It was a good era for a young folk musician to learn the intricacies, one might even say the responsibilities, of the tradition. The musical climate in the city of Dublin at the time did not encourage short-cuts or suggest easy options. There was certainly no promise of instant fame nor hope of financial success.

Rita Moloney, who has long since adapted to the life of being the wife of a professional musician frequently on world tours, remembers an incident in their courtship days when financial reward was an infrequent inducement to play music in public. On one occasion Paddy let her down by not arriving at the appointed place, Clery's clock in O'Connell Street, to take her to the cinema. He did, however, persuade his mother to go along and explain that he had been asked out of the blue to play at a function in Strokestown, County Roscommon, far from Dublin. This explanation she found less than satisfactory. Thereupon her future mother-in-law mentioned that he had been offered £2 for the engagement.

Rita still admits that this more or less stopped her in her tracks. At the time such a sum represented a hefty proportion of the average pay-packet. £2 for playing music for a couple of hours! Maybe, she thought, just maybe: there might be some sense to this music business after all.

In Manchester, 1977, shortly after Kevin joined the band   MANCHESTER DAILY MAIL

3 Early Days

The birth of the Chieftains was not due to some process akin to spontaneous combustion. Most of the original members of the group which got together in 1963 were already well known to each other as musicians and friends. Paddy Moloney met flute player Michael Tubridy as far back as the mid 1950s when the two established a strong musical connection, frequently performing together in concerts and making a number of radio programmes. Like Paddy, Michael also played the tin whistle as well as the concertina, an instrument closely associated with his native county of Clare.

In the Summer of 1956 the two took themselves off to Clare for a cycling holiday. They also brought along their instruments, with

Leo Rowsome conducting his school of young pipers in 1947. Paddy is second from the left.

The first fleadh ceoil in 1951 held in Mullingar – and also Paddy's first long trousers (extreme left)

the result that the whole venture developed into something of a grand musical tour. Many opportunities arose to play with local musicians, some of whom were relations of Michael's. In Milltown Malbay, after a long musical session with Willie Clancy and Martin Talty, they stayed at Jimmy Ward's guest-house in a room already occupied by four other customers. In the dead of night Paddy was summoned by a call of nature but was unable to locate the appropriate office as he didn't wish to turn on the light to awaken the slumberers. After a fruitless search of the entire premises he was reduced to opening the bedroom window. It would seem that no-one passed by below.

It was in 1959 that Paddy met whistle player Seán Potts. Seán's grandfather, originally from Wexford, set up residence in Dublin at Number 6, The Coombe. Soon the house became one of the best known gathering places for musicians in the city. His uncle, Tommy Potts, was and is among the most brilliant and indivi-dualistic traditional fiddlers in Ireland. Paddy was enthralled by his playing and used to make a point of going to hear him at the Church Street Club. He comments that, 'Even to listen to him fingering his instrument prior to tuning was in itself extra-ordinary.'

The sympathetic musical relationship between Paddy and Seán has been well documented in their joint *Tin Whistles* album, issued in 1973. Yet from the time when they first became acquainted the two used constantly to bounce musical ideas off each other, working out arrangements, experimenting with harmony, intro-ducing counter melody, and indulging in the odd bit of improvis-ation. Albeit unconsciously, the foundations for the musical philosophy of the Chieftains were being laid.

In 1959, the flute player and step dancer Paidí Bán Ó Broin invited Paddy and Seán, along with Charlie Tyndall, to come and spend a holiday in Connemara where he was teaching. They stayed in Spiddal in a single room and for each of them the vacation turned out to be a long session of uninhibited music-making, playing the nights away and drinking gallons of pineapple juice.

Back in Dublin, Paddy played in a quartet with Mick Tubridy, Jack Dervan, and Anne Walsh. Anne was a pianist, who, with Paddy, won a feis ceoil duet award. The combination of pipes and piano may seem unusual, yet the piece proved so popular that it was played by Ciarán MacMathúna for something like fourteen consecutive weeks on a well-known radio programme. A less typical association was his involvement in the Three Squares, a skiffle group formed largely to perform at the then annual Guinness concert.

At another stage he worked with a second quartet which included Martin Fay and Barney McKenna. Martin, like Seán and Mick, was of course to become a Chieftain, although Barney's career went in a different direction. He was once heard to remark, 'I should have been a Chieftain, but instead I grew the beard and became a Dubliner.'

Many of the Chieftains' fans might be surprised to realise that the institution of the ceili band played a part in Paddy's earlier musical experiences. He was involved in no less than two such bands, the Shannonside and the Loch Gamhna which also in-cluded Éamon de Buitléar, Seán Bracken, and Tony MacMahon. In later times much of his musical energy was devoted to developing a traditional ensemble sound, free from what he saw as the inhibiting qualities of the average ceili band: in fact the sound which has since become totally identified with the Chieftains. None the less he concedes that playing ceili music could be

The Three Squares, who performed at the Guinness annual concert in the mid 1950s

T. MOLLOY

27

enjoyable, and still refers to a guest appearance with the famous Tulla band as an 'honour'.

Through his various musical associations, at this stage of his life Paddy was making regular and frequent professional appearances. Yet in those days there was no possibility of music alone providing a basic living. On leaving school he joined the staff of Baxendales, one of the largest firms of builders' providers in the country, and remained with them for some twelve years working mainly in the accounting department.

Working for a large commercial concern did not prove a disagreeable experience, with rapid promotion leading to a middle-management position. The company proved receptive to new ideas and Paddy was pleased that some of his own suggested schemes for departmental reorganisation were adopted both by the Dublin office and also the parent company in Manchester. With hindsight it was also a useful period, giving him the opportunity to develop business skills which were in time to prove invaluable.

Baxendales were reasonably tolerant in accommodating the requirements of a member of staff who was also a part-time professional musician. But it is doubtful whether the company would have given its whole-hearted approval to a stroke which Paddy, along with Éamon de Buitléar, pulled on a regular basis.

Éamon was of course to become a celebrated film-maker specialising in wildlife subjects, as well as forming his own

The Three Squares in another versatile act!

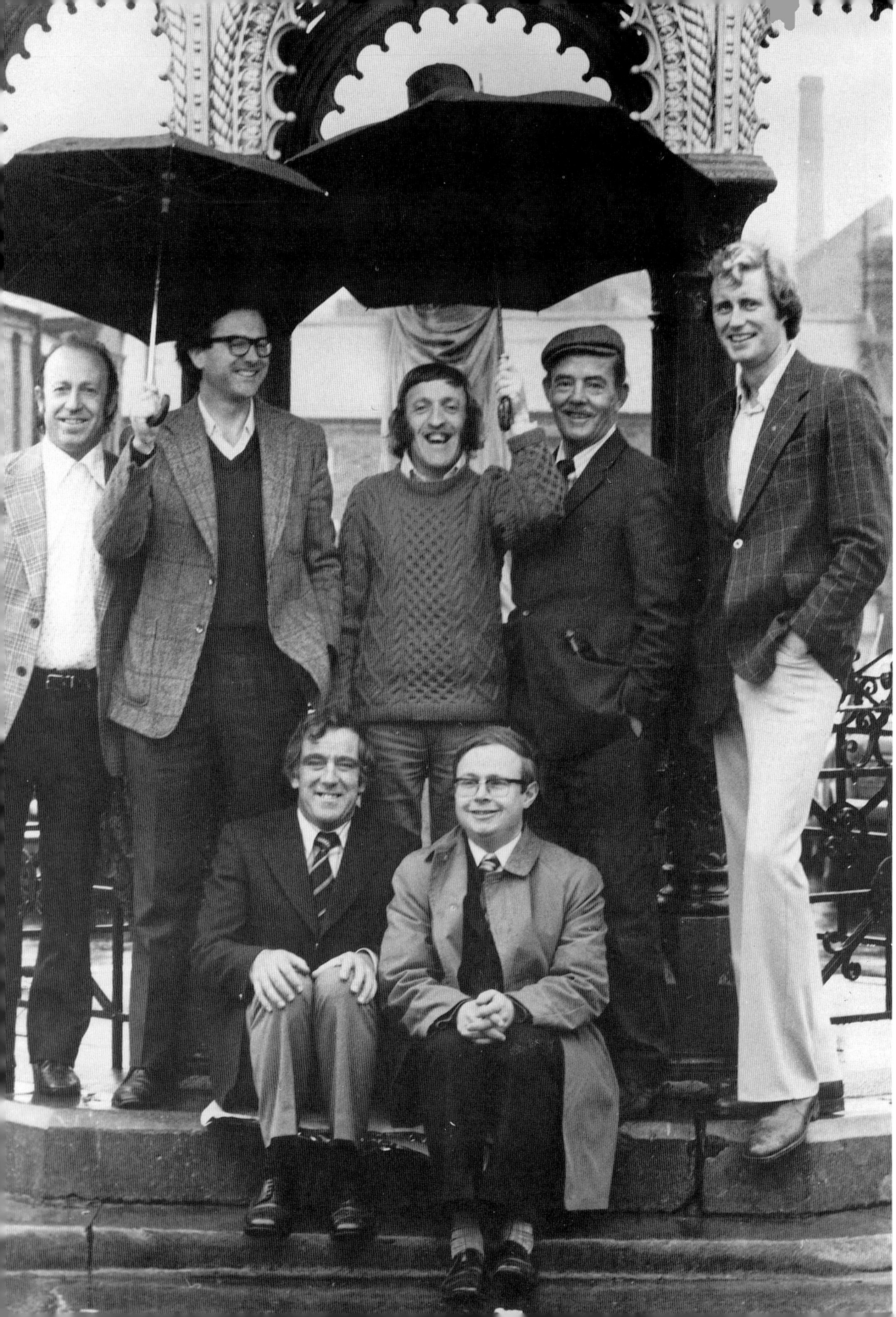

CLADDAGH RECORDS

Seán Ó Riada

traditional ensemble, Ceoltóirí Laigheann. However at that time he worked in the sports section of Hely's department store, even if his media career had already begun. On a weekly basis he presented a radio programme for children in the late afternoon from the Henry Street studios of Radio Éireann. The station was close to his place of employ, as it was to Paddy's, who used to join him on the show to illustrate particular points on the pipes and whistle. The only problem was that, unknown to both sets of employers, the show went out live during standard office hours. Paddy recollects, 'When the programme was over I had to hurry back to clock out on time, clutching a batch of special pens which could only be obtained at Hely's.' This touch was to convince his employers that he had been gainfully occupied during his absence.

It was Éamon who introduced Paddy to the composer Seán Ó Riada, who used to call to Hely's to purchase fishing tackle. He was already well aware of the piper's reputation as a musician, and

A 1974 photograph taken in the Liberties of Dublin

from the very start of their friendship took a keen interest in the younger man. At one stage he even suggested that he use his influence to have Paddy recruited as a piper into the Radio Éireann Light Orchestra. The plan was never pursued, although had it materialised such a development would have been revolutionary for the time.

Ó Riada was in the process of becoming one of the best-known Irishmen of his era. He was born in Cork in 1931, and after a youth spent in County Limerick returned to the city of his birth to study music under Professor Aloys Fleischmann. On his graduation he was appointed assistant director of music in Radio Éireann, but relinquished the post less than two years' later to pursue further studies chiefly in Italy and France. It was through his continental musical associations that he became influenced by the twelve-tone-row approach to composition as pioneered by Schoenberg. Although his output of composition in this vein was not extensive, he is none the less regarded as a significant contributor to twentieth-century Irish orchestral music.

On returning to Ireland Ó Riada was appointed musical director to the Abbey Theatre, an office which entailed arranging and conducting Irish airs for small orchestra. In 1960 Gael Linn, the Irish language organisation, released George Morrison's film *Mise Éire*, which through brilliant use of archive material portrayed in documentary form the events leading to the foundation of the Irish state. Ó Riada had been invited to provide the musical score, and his response established him as a composer of programme music of exceptional merit. The reaction of the public was unprecedented. Somehow the music managed to express the most deeply-felt national aspirations and Seán Ó Riada, quite simply, became a household name.

Among the many to be moved by the evocation and colour of the *Mise Éire* score was Paddy Moloney. He saw the film shortly after its release at the Regal Cinema and was immediately drawn to the orchestral setting of traditional themes. Ó Riada was already at that time engrossed with the grand design of rediscovering his traditional musical roots, and consciously resolved to seek out the company of authentic traditional musicians. One of those with whom he was to become closely associated was Paddy Moloney.

The poet John Montague has described a boisterous evening of music-making during which Ó Riada slapped Paddy on the back to declare him 'the best musicianer in Ireland'. The incident typifies the intense professional relationship between the two, a relationship which could be stormy and even competitive. Paddy still remembers the sparks flying when he and Seán, playing fiddle on this occasion, vied with each other to produce spontaneous variations on 'The Blackbird'. No variation was permitted repetition and in all they worked their way through the tune twenty-six times.

The Chieftains in 1975 at Luggala, Co. Wicklow

At the Snape Maltings, Suffolk in 1981

At a festival in Macroom, early 1970s

But perhaps his most poignant memory stems from a time shortly before Seán's death. The two had just completed a hard-working recording session at Garech a Brún's residence at Luggala. The assignment had been the taping of Ó Riada's recital on the upright harpsichord, the clavicytheriam. On arrival in Dublin they stopped and chatted in the car prior to Seán's departure on the train to Cork. 'At the time he looked desperately ill. But he had a fatherly talk with me, asked how I was getting on, and seemed pleased that I was determined to continue seriously with music.'

Later Paddy, along with Ioan Allen, put in a lot of work editing that session. The instrument had been badly in need of repair and the process actually involved substituting notes from elsewhere on the tape. It meant a great deal to him that Seán expressed deep satisfaction with the finished product which he heard while literally on his death bed. It was eventually released by Claddagh as *Ó Riada's Farewell*.

But back in 1960 Ó Riada's thoughts were far from death: on the contrary, he was on the threshold of one of the most productive and acclaimed periods of his life. The house in which he and his wife Ruth lived at Galloping Green in South County Dublin, became a regular venue for evenings not only of music but also dancing, singing, and a vast amount of poetry in both Irish and English. Pleasant that these occasions were, Seán saw them as leading to something more than social diversion. From the traditional musicians who gathered there, he envisaged a permanent folk ensemble or even orchestra emerging. A group which would confidently tackle arrangements, harmony, and even improvisation but at the same time feature only accepted traditional instruments.

What in fact did emerge was Ceoltóirí Cualann, consisting of Martin Fay and John Kelly on fiddles, Paddy Moloney on pipes and whistle, Michael Tubridy on flute, Éamon de Buitléar and Sonny Brogan on accordions, Ronnie McShane on bones, with Seán Ó Riada playing bodhrán as well as acting as musical director. In time, Ó Riada augmented the ensemble by introducing the harpsichord in the belief that it more closely related to the ancient Irish *cruit* than did the neo-Irish harp.

There were other recruits to the Ceoltóirí. The fiddlers were joined by Seán Keane after he won a national instrumental radio award; and by Peadar Mercier, who like some of the other members was already involved with Paddy in a further group, and who took over the bodhrán. Ó Riada also called on the talents of two singers, Darach Ó Catháin who sang in the *sean-nós* and the tenor Seán Ó Sé.

Despite a variety of musical backgrounds and apart from the odd clash, the combination worked well and Paddy still recalls the atmosphere as being that of a 'happy family': indeed Seán Ó Riada played at his wedding, substituting a traditional tune for the more usual 'Wedding March'. Although not officially titled Ceoltóirí Cualann at that stage, the ensemble first went public at the Abbey Theatre with Bryan MacMahon's play *The Golden Folk*. Rehearsals had a habit of developing into sessions, with the same thing happening at the fall of the final curtain. A father-figure of the Irish theatre, Harry Brogan, used to sit enthralled during all of this and small wonder, for in his time his father had been a pipe-maker and musician.

The first four years of the 1960s were spectacular for the Ceoltóirí. There was virtually no touring and surprisingly few concerts, yet the ensemble became nationally known through the two radio series *Reacaireacht an Riadaigh* and *Fleadh Cheoil an Radio*. There was always a carefree and happy attitude towards the music despite the underlying idealistic motivation.

The director and the members of the group had a give-and-take working relationship. The instrumentalists introduced Seán to

Paddy's first trip abroad – to the Celtic festival in Brittany, 1961

much of the material, airs as well as dance tunes, while he gave to them a great deal which they found new, especially song/airs which he had gathered in the Gaeltacht. Two Gael Linn albums capture the atmosphere of the period, *Reacaireacht an Riadaigh* named for the radio series, and *Ceol na nUasal,* the music of the nobles.

Ó Riada wished to highlight the surviving works of the seventeenth and eighteenth-century harper/composers, especially those of Carolan. Paddy Moloney too had long admired this type of music and was saddened that it received relatively little attention from contemporary Irish musicians, let alone audiences. His own interest in Carolan in particular stemmed from his tuition with Leo Rowsome. As a youngster the famous 'Concerto' had quickly become a party piece, and Leo had taught him pieces attributed to the harper such as 'Blind Mary' and 'Planxty Davis'. To this day, among his most cherished possessions are the two volumes on the life of Carolan by Donal O'Sullivan, given to him in 1959 by his sister Esther as a twenty-first birthday present.

He also discovered common ground with Ó Riada in his approach to instrumental arrangement, for this too had fascinated him from the time he had started to play with other musicians, indeed back to his schooldays. And yet he still nourished the ambition to put together an ensemble with a distinctive sound somewhat different to that of the Ceoltóirí.

In 1961 Ceoltóirí Cualann provided the musical backing for the film version of *The Playboy of the Western World,* featuring Siobhán McKenna. As a member of the group, it was for Paddy the first of many involvements with this particular play. In times since he has worked on ballet, television, and straight theatre versions of the drama and has come to regard it with almost a proprietorial attitude.

From 1964 Ceoltóirí Cualann ceased to play with any regularity, although as late as 1969 it did record two excellent live albums on the occasion of a concert to commemorate the bi-centenary of the poet Peadar Ó Doirnín; these were issued by Gael Linn as *Ó Riada 'sa Gaiety* and the other simply *Ó Riada.*

Seán himself had taken up an academic appointment at University College Cork in 1963, and at the same time brought his family to live in the Gaeltacht area of Cúil Aodha. Before the end of the decade he publicly announced the dissolution of the group.

Although he himself was heavily committed to the Chieftains at that stage, Paddy telephoned Ó Riada in the early hours of the morning to ask him to reconsider his decision. But to no avail. It would seem that he felt that he had fulfilled his contribution to Irish traditional ensemble music.

Seán Ó Riada died in a London hospital in October 1971. Apart from the many who knew him as a friend, his death was mourned throughout Ireland and beyond. None grieved his passing more than his former comrades in Ceoltóirí Cualann.

Regular observers of the Chieftains on stage may sometimes wonder why it is that for no obvious reason the entire band appears to be on the verge of bursting out in a collective fit of uncontrollable laughter. Invariably the answer is due to some devastating remark uttered ever so softly by one of the gentlemen fiddlers, Mr Martin Fay. By all appearances Martin is the quiet man of the ensemble and quiet he is, but he is also possessed of an acute sense of humour. Apart from the MD, he is the sole member of the group of five musicians who gathered in Moloney's of Milltown in 1963 still to serve as a full-time Chieftain.

His love for music dates back to his earliest years. While still a boy growing up in

*Award of Gold Disc for
Best Folk Album in Spain,
1973*

Dublin he was taken to a film on the life of Paganini. This was the moment of truth.
From then on there was no doubt that whatever else life brought, he was going to be a
violinist. As it turned out from the first stages of his musical education, it was obvious
that there was an exceptional talent on which to build such an ambition. His training
proceeded along classical lines, with a dedication to hard work being recognised by an
appointment to the small orchestra attached to the Abbey Theatre. He was still then a
very young man and saw no reason to give up his studies because of this commitment.
Serious practice continued and resulted in a scholarship to the Municipal School of
Music in Dublin.

Seán Ó Riada, who was of course director of music at the Abbey, quickly recognised
Martin's outstanding ability. This led to a further association by way of an invitation
to join Ceoltóirí Cualann and also getting to know Paddy Moloney. It was no more
than the natural progression of events that he should have eventually become a
founding member of the Chieftains.

Although his training was formal, Martin has always shown a natural understanding of traditional music. This is never more obvious than when he is interpreting
one of the great song airs on the fiddle. Often in concerts it falls to him to lead an
audience from a mood of boisterous vivacity into one of tranquillity and silent emotion.
As a musician he is above all a great stylist.

For Martin, becoming a full-time Chieftain was a decision not taken lightly. His
employment did not allow for the luxury of a period of secondment to buy time to see
what the future might bring. But then, as now, all his instincts were those of the true
'pro', and today his colleagues will testify that he is the perfect companion on the road
and almost oblivious to the strains that arise in the course of lengthy tours.
Widespread recognition has done nothing to alter his modesty and good humour.
Travel seems to agree with him, and yet he loves to get home. He cites one of his
favourite pleasures as having a jar in his favourite pub in the company of good friends.
Martin is married to the well-known dancer Gertie McCormack and they have two
children.

5 *On the Road*

Confusion has sometimes arisen regarding the relationship of Ceoltóirí Cualann and the Chieftains, due to a number of the musicians having dual membership of both ensembles. In fact for quite a long period the two groups operated simultaneously.

In 1963 Garech a Brún, who had founded Claddagh Records some four years earlier, asked Paddy to get together a number of musicians for the purpose of making a long playing record. His response was to enlist the talents of Michael Tubridy, Seán Potts, and Martin Fay. These four musicians could between them build an instrumental range to include pipes, three tin whistles, fiddle, flute, and concertina. Percussion was introduced in the person of Davey Fallon, a friend of Garech's from Castletown Geoghan who was an accomplished hand on the bodhrán. In the course of a session at Davey's home Paddy had quickly realised that he was just the man they needed to provide the rhythm section for the album.

After Paddy arranged about forty minutes' music for the recording, the group got down to rehearsing the pieces intensively. All the musicians had day jobs so normally these practice sessions were held in the evening, with the music rendering everyone oblivious to the passage of time. Well, not quite everyone. Rita Moloney's grandfather, known to the family as Pappa, made it a habit to interrupt proceedings at about 10.40 each night by flashing a torch at the face of a venerable old wall clock. His point was that there weren't very many minutes left for those dry from all the music-making and in need of a quick pint before closing time.

Again because of work commitments, the recording sessions were also held outside office hours at the Peter Hunt Studios. Frequently the atmosphere was splendidly informal, with numerous well-known musicians such as the 'Gabe' O'Sullivan and Martin Byrnes, who were not themselves involved in the taping, dropping by to see what was going on.

One of Paddy's plans for the disc was to have a troupe of dancers tap out the rhythm of the tunes. The idea was not so eccentric as it might seem, for this formula had been the basis of a successful radio series. At least to emulate the effect, Morgan O'Sullivan, then a sound engineer with Peter Hunt, tried rigging up a sheet of hardboard; however the idea was abandoned due to technical problems. But some thirteen years and many records later this particular ambition was fulfilled with the release of *Bonaparte's*

Michael Tubridy at Coolfin in his native Co. Clare

41

RTE

Retreat, on a track entitled 'Around the House and Mind the Dresser'.

With the tracks taped, the editing completed, and the sleeve notes written by Seán MacReamoinn, there remained the problem that the group had as yet no name to serve as title for the album. Many years later John Montague, himself a director of Claddagh, was to recall, 'We named them after a book of mine which had just appeared.' Such indeed was the case. The book in question was *Death of a Chieftain* which is perhaps ironical in that the naming of the group had rather more to do with *birth*.

With the release of the disc Paddy was giving notice that he had found the 'sound' which he had been seeking. It was a carefully structured sound — anchored to the base of the drones and cascading upwards through the weave of fiddle, flute, and whistle, whilst propelled onwards by the pulse of the skin of a goat. He still regards the launching of the disc as a crucial moment in the band's career. '1963 was the year when the distinctive sound of the Chieftains finally emerged: the foundations were laid for what the Chieftains have become today.'

In future times he was to build on the sound, but always with a degree of caution. The instrumentation has since been augmented to add greater body and colour to the weave, nevertheless the essential quality of that sound has been preserved. Admirers of the Chieftains would have it no other way. From the start the album was exceptionally well received, but this did not mean that widespread fame was its instant reward.

The first Chieftains' album sold at a rate of hundreds rather than thousands per annum. It is a measure of the subsequent development of the Irish recording industry that at that time these sales were regarded as very favourable. The group had assembled with the specific purpose of making one recording, but in the making it established itself as a permanent feature on the traditional music scene, even if the measure of permanence could not then have been foreseen.

In the immediate years after the release of *Chieftains I,* it became increasingly obvious that more and more people wanted to hear more and more of the sound, live as well as on their turntables. At first public appearances were not frequent, but gradually the bookings came in, although this process was selective and vetted. Paddy was determined that he and his colleagues should only perform at venues where they would be heard to good advantage. But audiences were continuing to grow.

Even prior to being established on the international circuit, the Chieftains seemed to catch the attention of a great many people prominent in every aspect of the entertainment business. Peter O'Toole was an early fan, given to expressing appreciation in his

Seán Ó Riada with the Ceoltóirí Cualann in an RTE studio in the mid 1960s

43

own characteristic manner. At a reception in Eamonn Andrews'
house he silenced a perfectly melodious gypsy ensemble to insist the
Chieftains take the stage. On another occasion he threw his boot
through the air during a party to demand total attention for the
musicians.

It was due to director John Huston that the Chieftains once
found themselves half way up a mountain playing before a
gathering of distinguished film folk. This was during the making of
Sinful Davey; in breaks in location on Calary Bog in County
Wicklow he sometimes provided entertainment for the cast. His
daughter Angelica led the dance on that occasion — and no better
woman, being herself a member of the Georgian Dance Company.

Mick Jagger and Marianne Faithful were another pair to make
early acquaintance with the band, showing real appreciation for
the music at an evening arranged at Castletown House in County
Kildare. Presumably neither Jagger nor Moloney thought to
contemplate that both Stones and Chieftains would someday
appear on the same bill. All that would come to pass many years
later.

As concert engagements continued to increase, so too did media
appearances. The first television programme was in 1965 on Ulster
Television, with the group dashing to Dublin immediately after
the show in Belfast to take part in a function celebrating the first
Golden Harp, an annual Eurovision festival of folk music and lore
hosted by Radio Telefís Éireann. This was the only live public
occasion that Davey Fallon, then in his late seventies, played with
the band. His replacement by Peadar Mercier came not long
afterwards.

The rise of the Chieftains in the Irish popularity stakes began to
be reflected in England and Scotland. From 1967 they received
positive and useful attention from key media people in Britain,
especially John Peel and Wally Whytton. Peel in particular was
noted for giving them generous coverage on his influential BBC
show. Even in those early years it was already clear that a new force
had been launched into the world of entertainment.

I personally will never forget hearing them for the first time in a
fairly large arena. I cannot precisely remember the date, but I do
know that I had been engaged by a daily newspaper to cover the
event. Admittedly I went along predisposed to enjoy myself. Being
involved in the business I was already familiar with the work of the
band and of its individual members. To me their first album had
been the most exciting group recording of Irish instrumental music
ever to come my way. I had also already heard them in public
performance but only in more intimate surroundings. The
experience of witnessing the Chieftains at large in the environment
of an auditorium was something different, something for which I
was not totally prepared.

From the word go I noticed that the audience itself was

The original Ceoltóirí Cualann in 1961

uncharacteristic. Covering folk concerts gives one a nose for audiences, and this one was representative of strata of the community wider than that normally given to patronising traditional events. As the people gathered there was an air of subdued expectancy. Then the musicians made their way onto the stage to a round of applause, friendly rather than ecstatic. So far nothing unusual. Paddy spoke a few words of welcome and straightaway the music began. That was the moment when it all started to happen.

The first item was a selection of fast dance tunes and immediately an extraordinary chemistry took over: not mass hysteria so much as mass involvement. I had never witnessed so many become so rapidly engrossed in what was happening on the stage. And this was *traditional* music! The atmosphere was different from anything previously experienced. Different from the high emotion shown at pop concerts, often engendered by gimmicks. Different too from the rapt but silent attention displayed at orchestral recitals. There were no gimmicks, and the attention if rapt was certainly far from silent. *The music was speaking for itself,* but the crowd was going mad. Yet happily mad. There was no ugliness, no hint of any unpleasant element to intrude on this amazing communion between artists and audience.

A publicity shot of the group in the late 1970s

With a change of metre, so changed the mood of the multitude. A slow air played simply and movingly now reduced us to total silence. Whatever the secret of their spell the Chieftains had us eating out of their hands, and lovingly. Thus they plied our emotions up to the moment when they broke into a final wild reel, a signal for some to abandon their seats and leap in the aisles. Thereafter one last roof-elevating roar of valediction.

In the cold light of aftermath I remember, pen in hand, trying vainly to get on with the job I had been asked to do. But how to describe the atmosphere surrounding that night's work without resorting to the most abused of clichés: 'electric', 'charismatic', 'sensational.' These were the words that jumped to mind.

Far from the roar of the crowd, at an early stage in the career of the group Paddy began to receive assignments to arrange programme music, initially for short television documentaries such as *I'm a stranger here myself.* It was the beginning of a side of his professional life which was to assume increasing importance with the passing of time. But if 1963 had been a crucial period in his life, then so too was 1968. The Chieftains were becoming widely acclaimed and although there was no immediate question of the band turning full-time, it did seem a good moment to take stock of what was happening. For Paddy this was more than a theoretical exercise when Garech a Brún invited him to resign from Baxendales to take on the job of managing Claddagh Records.

The decision was difficult, for he had already long assumed family responsibilities having married Rita O'Reilly, the daughter of a dynasty of stonemasons, back in the year when the group was formed. But eventually, with Rita's support, he accepted.

The relationship between Paddy, the Chieftains, and Claddagh is related in greater detail elsewhere (see *Black Wax*). Suffice it to say that the job was challenging. The company, founded on idealism, operated on a tiny profit with a catalogue of only a few titles. To this day he remains proud of the role he played in its development; and of the fact that when he amicably resigned his position as managing director some years later to devote all his time to the group, Claddagh was not only viable but had a large and varied catalogue.

On another level that year was also important, for it brought the Chieftains to the Edinburgh Festival, the first of many visits. Unfortunately Seán Potts and Martin were unable to take part due to a long-term commitment, however it was at this stage that Seán Keane joined the band permanently. The Festival provided a good opportunity to launch the album seriously on the British market, and such was the response that it became clear that a successor would have to be recorded.

Chieftains 2 was in fact made in Edinburgh the following year, by which time Seán Potts and Martin Fay were again firmly established in the regular line-up. The celebrated Gaelic scholar

Paddy with his close friend Hugh Mac Diarmid in Dublin, 1973

and collector, Seán O Boyle, greeted the new album poetically:

> Heavenly King if I'd only the fingers
> You gave to the piper to strike up a tune
> I'd make music so charming
> We'd all leave the farm
> And go singing and dancing
> From morning to noon.

He went on to explain his choice of verse: 'The unknown Gaelic poet whose words I have adapted would most certainly have welcomed this second offering from the Chieftains. Poetry and music, piping, fiddling, fluting, singing, and dancing were for him the stuff of life and they are the stuff of this record.'

This time the album was well received in Europe and America as well as Britain and Ireland. It also marked the continued development of the group, as it included elaborate arrangements such as 'The Fox Chase'. Paddy made his first trip to the United States to promote the disc, but also took the opportunity to tour as a solo musician.

Musical commitments were now beginning to create difficulties with the day jobs of individual Chieftains, especially the two Seáns who were both in the public service. Problems arose such as whether requests for unpaid leave would affect pension rights — important considerations to family men. Valuable assistance in this regard was given by the then Chief Justice, Cearbhall Ó Dálaigh, in his capacity as a member of the government-sponsored Cultural Affairs Committee.

The Chief Justice maintained an interest in the band even after his eventual inauguration as President of Ireland. He often appeared at press conferences declaring that he would be gone after a quick cup of tea, only to be discovered two hours later still discussing the music in his animated fashion. As Paddy testifies, 'He was a lovely man.'

In 1970 the band received a spectacular reception when it appeared at a concert in Dublin's National Stadium featuring the group Fairport Convention. This confirmed that the appeal of the Chieftains was extending to an audience far beyond traditional enthusiasts. The same message came clearly from a performance compered by John Peel in Wexford with Earth, Wind, and Fire, an outfit whose musical range encompassed rock, Caribbean elements, and some contemporary jazz. On the other end of the popular music spectrum, at a further concert an audience was pleased to accept both the Chieftains and the middle-of-the-road singer Roger Whittaker.

The many opportunities of being professionally associated with

FOTO FELICI

Meeting the Pope in January 1980

48

prominent musicians from all sorts of musical backgrounds were providing the Chieftains with useful experience as well as playing a part in bringing their work before a widely-based public. This was not without its dangers. Numerous promoters in the business believed that, given a degree of musical compromise, the Chieftains could be manipulated to become rapidly a highly marketable commodity. Many such suggestions were made to Paddy, especially with the advent of 'folk rock' as a popular form. Consistently and adamantly, he opposed the notion of the band

A rare photograph showing the Ceoltóirí Cualann in tails at the Gaiety Theatre concert

moving in such a direction: 'I always believed that if we waited long enough and remained true to ourselves and to our music, we would achieve our goals.'

The growing popularity of the band was already having a welcome spin-off effect on record sales. *Chieftains 2* was marketing well but so too was the first album. The management of Claddagh decided that the future policy of the company should include further albums featuring the group, to be issued at regular intervals. In line with this, *Chieftains 3* was recorded in London in 1971, the choice of venue dictated by the availability of good

Paddy Moloney

Martin Fay

Seán Keane

Kevin Conneff

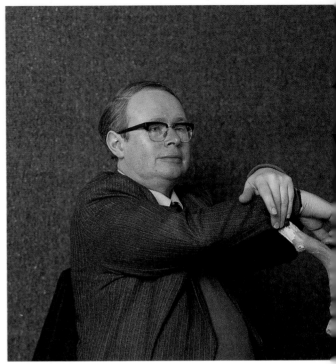

Derek Bell

Matt Molloy

technical facilities. One track highlighted the lilting of Pat Kilduff. At a live concert he had once held the people in their seats during the entire interval, accompanied only by the bodhrán of Peadar Mercier. In his sleeve notes Seán MacReamoinn wrote of the inventiveness of the recording, inventive but 'always faithful to the *dúchas*, the natural integrity of the music'. The international appeal of the record was highlighted two years later with the award of a Spanish golden disc by the Bienal Internacional del Sonido, Valladolid, 1973.

Seán and Derek

The elusive ensemble sound which Paddy had always striven for, almost since childhood, had essentially been established since the practice sessions prior to the recording of the first album. Yet almost a decade later he still felt that there was an ingredient missing. In short, the harp.

In 1972 Alan Tongue, the television director, invited the group to record a version of Carolan's 'Concerto' with the BBC Northern Ireland Orchestra. The orchestral harper was Derek Bell, and after the performance he agreed to make a number of guest appearances with the Chieftains playing mostly Carolan pieces. Almost immediately Paddy knew in his bones that 'the introduction of the harp completed the sound which I had always wanted to achieve'.

One thing led to another and within two years Derek had become a fully-fledged Chieftain, participating in virtually all performances. He did not, however, immediately sever his connection with the BBC which led to difficulties in arranging his schedule. Once he approached a senior member of the corporation to seek sanction for yet another spell of unscheduled leave, explaining his proposed absence as being due to a concert of exceptional importance. The response was sorrowful rather than angry: 'Derek! When are you going to give up that tatty folk group?'

The presence of Derek added enrichment to the fourth album which was recorded in London in 1974. The tracks included the extended suite 'The Battle of Aughrim' and 'The Morning Dew', two of the most enduring and popular items ever performed by the band. So much so that the latter was released as a single, backed by 'The Tip of the Whistle', Moloney's arrangement of the harp composition 'Molly St George'. This single found its way into the Irish general charts, while the LP topped the *Melody Maker* folk charts.

On the sleeve there is an account of a party in the course of which the writer met Paddy: 'Whenever I listen to this Chieftains LP it unlocks a door in my mind, and the memory comes flooding back. Paddy, please keep making records like this for folk like me and The Milligan, and the millions.' The writer was Peter Sellers. Some years later he attempted to set up what would have been the most unusual, not to say eccentric, photo-call in history. He planned to fly the Chieftains to London in order to photograph them in the Orange Garden in Regent's Park. At the last moment he postponed the engagement, having reorganised his day to get married instead. The photo-call was mooted to take place at a later date but unfortunately the great leveller intervened. On the night that Sellers died, Paddy had a strange psychic experience. He woke up at about 1.30 in the morning to see Peter standing at the end of his bed, in exactly the same posture as he had first been introduced to him at Carton. Later, on the 8 o'clock news, he was to learn that he had died.

One of the pieces on *Chieftains 4* was 'Mná na hÉireann', an instrumental interpretation of Ó Riada's song setting of Ó Doirnín's poem which Paddy arranged by way of tribute to his late friend. It so happened that the piece was heard by film director Stanley Kubrick who decided he would like to incorporate it into the score of his forthcoming production *Barry Lyndon*. This was accomplished sometime later and eventually the score was awarded an Oscar.

A cherubic Derek Bell in 1974

As the year progressed, 1974 became increasingly hectic for the members of a band still operating on a part-time basis. As well as

Paddy at home in Milltown with (from left) Aonghus, Aedín (on her first communion day), grandfather O'Neill and wife Rita. This was taken in 1974.

radio and television work there was a plethora of festivals and tours, not only in Ireland but also Britain and Europe, and in addition a two-week trip to the west coast of the United States. During this, unexpected support appeared in the form of Jerry Garcia, leader of the Grateful Dead. Perhaps it was something of a surprise to find an admirer of the Chieftains so identified with the anti-establishment rock culture of California, but life was increasingly full of surprises. The contact with him led to an impromptu concert along with some members of the Dead, and a lengthy appearance on one of the West Coast's most highly-rated chat shows in which the Irish musicians and Garcia were jointly interviewed.

The year also brought Paddy another unusual musical experience when he travelled to Stockport in Cheshire to accompany Mick McGear of Scaffold, on an album produced by McGear's brother the former Beatle Paul McCartney. Afterwards he maintained contact with McCartney and his wife Linda although it was six years before they again met professionally. Paul invited Paddy to contribute a solo passage on pipes to 'Rainclouds', the flip side to his 'Ebony and Ivory' single made in conjunction with Stevie Wonder. Just before leaving for London, Paddy heard the ghastly news that John Lennon had been murdered and at once expected the session to be cancelled. But despite the tragedy, in the age old spirit of the business Paul and his producer George Martin decided to carry on. It was none the less a strange recording, perfectly business-like, but punctuated by many friends dropping in to the studio to share the grief.

Early in 1975 Paddy, along with Pat Pretty, represented Claddagh at the Midem Festival in Cannes, an important showcase for the recording industry. The occasion had its lighter moments. Lady Oranmore and Browne, Garech a Brún's mother, accorded them the hospitality of a villa at Antibes, complete with Vietnamese chef, so Paddy decided to organise a hooley Irish-style. Being the only musician present he happily played the pipes for much of the evening, but at a later stage abandoned the instrument to join the dance, specifically in the company of the actress Charlotte Rampling. This, one is reliably informed, was recorded on camera yet by all accounts to this day Rita has been unable to unearth the evidence.

On a more serious level, many of the people he met at the Festival suggested that the time was ripe for the Chieftains to take on international management, and that Claddagh should investigate the advantages of international distribution. Indirectly this advice led to discussions with the American impressario Jo Lustig.

Lustig was a larger-than-life character, professionally aggressive but always prepared to rise to the challenge. His managerial experience included handling artists and groups such as Steeleye Span, Fairport Convention, the Pentangle, Mary O'Hara, Mel Tormé, and John Cassavetes. When he eventually took over the Chieftains' portfolio, friction sometimes arose, especially when he would try to persuade the group to forgo a period of agreed domestic tranquillity to take on some unexpected engagement. Once on the telephone when he was answered by Paddy's daughter Aedín, he demanded to speak to her father.

'Who's on the line?' asked Paddy.

'Jaws!' replied Aedín.

Despite the inevitable clash of temperament, there is no question that he was the right man for the Chieftains at that point in their careers. When he eventually parted company with the group after about two years, they were already well established as international artists. Thereafter Paddy was to assume the dual role of manager and musical director for a lengthy period which proved an intolerable burden. In the interim, two different managers were engaged for limited periods, but it was only in comparatively recent times that this function was delegated to Joe Whitston, long the Chieftains' legal adviser and trusted by them all.

In practice, some of the managerial experiences evoke the least happy personal memories. In particular Paddy remembers a bleak winter's day when, during an airport stop-over, conversations with

separate members of the group suggested that the band was in imminent danger of losing a number of members all at once. It didn't work out that way, but it was a hell of a worrying thought to take home for Christmas.

The group outside Garech a Brún's home in Luggala, 1974

Shortly before arrangements were formalised with Lustig, Paddy telephoned his future manager with a request for assistance. The Chieftains were due to tour Britain, but no venue had been worked out for London which was their point of departure. Could Jo perhaps arrange a concert in some modestly equipped hall, something in the nature of a seven to eight hundred seater? A few days later Lustig returned his call.

'You won't believe it. I've got you a great concert.'

'Where?'

'The Albert Hall.'

'What? You must be joking!'

No joke, and despite terrifying reservations Paddy eventually allowed himself to be talked into what he believed to be a totally insane project. The Albert Hall! And only three weeks to put the publicity machine into operation! But into operation it went, with Moloney engaged in a rampage of promotional activity such as he had never experienced. But it paid off. On the big night the Chieftains walked on stage in the knowledge that the Albert Hall was filled to capacity.

Clearing that first hurdle did little to calm the nerves of the band who felt somewhat like footballers entering a vast sports arena. By the end of the evening the roar of the crowd was not unlike that of triumphant spectators at a cup final. In a sense the Chieftains were collectively numbed. It took time to digest that they had just accomplished their greatest triumph to date. Only after the last of countless encores was the dam of pent-up emotions finally released — tears as well as laughter.

The success at the Albert Hall was a catalyst. Now it was unavoidable that a decision which had been haunting Paddy and his colleagues would have to be faced. A decision to be made individually and collectively, for it touched on every aspect of their lives, both domestic and professional. There was much soul-searching and consultation, but finally the nettle was grasped: the Chieftains were going full-time.

Almost immediately the exuberance of the moment was dispelled by a period dominated by tiresome but necessary legalities. Long-term secondments were required for some members of the band, while contracts had to be negotiated between management and the Chieftains, the Chieftains and Claddagh, management and Claddagh, Claddagh and the various internationally oriented recording companies, and these companies and the Chieftains. It was complicated and even bewildering but eventually all interested parties gathered at a London venue in anticipation of a grand signing ceremony, along with representatives of the press. At last the legalities were completed. Or were they?

At the eleventh hour one small contractual clause had still to be settled between Paddy and Jo. Excusing themselves from the gathering they retired to an upstairs room to attempt to stitch up the deal to their mutual satisfaction. Time passed, and quite a lot of it, with the company at the reception below becoming increasingly aware of voices raised in argument in the room above. Suddenly the two returned, but in a stage of agitation.

'It's all off!'

And so it was. But not for long. Within days negotiations were finalised and the Chieftains constituted as a full-time professional band.

Going full-time was marked by a period of enormous activity, including a seventeen-concert tour of Britain which brought the Chieftains from the south of England to the north of Scotland. Paddy travelled the route ahead of the band, visiting every venue

in what proved an exhausting but worthwhile promotional exercise. He took one night off, when along with Jo Lustig he was invited to Mike Oldfield's house in Wales. There he recorded some piping for an album in the making, *Ommadawn*. The following morning Mike arranged their transport to Southampton, their next port-of-call, by way of private plane. Since that session the two musicians have maintained a professional relationship, including joint concert performances.

At Minnesota in 1981

Around this period everything went well. The British tour took in a second appearance at the Albert Hall, where once again the scenes of wild euphoria were repeated, and *Chieftains 5* was issued to establish itself quickly as a good seller featuring in both the UK and US charts. The album introduced Derek playing the timpan, his reconstructed version of an old Irish instrument of the psaltery family. Then, to top it all, the annual *Melody Maker* poll was published with the Chieftains voted 'Group of the Year'.

The end of the British tour left only five days before the band was due to set off for North America, so no one was overly enthusiastic when Stanley Kubrick phoned urgently with a request to come immediately to London to record extra music for *Barry Lyndon.* As it turned out, he dealt with the situation with flamboyant generosity by flying over not only the Chieftains but also their families, even laying on a magnificent fireworks display for the children.

The tour itself was something of a whirlwind, establishing a pace to which the musicians have since of necessity become accustomed. They played in the Avery Fisher Hall in New York and the Massey Hall in Toronto before winging on to Washington DC, San Francisco, and Los Angeles. The main reason why the trip was planned was promotion for the future and Paddy was deeply impressed by the professional skill and energy of his publicist and friend Charlie Comer, who in times since has continued to give the group the benefit of his experience. In all no less than forty television, press, and radio interviews were arranged.

The tour was hardly over when the band found itself back in New York at the beginning of 1976 for a marathon Irish celebrity concert featuring artists such as Siobhán McKenna, Peter O'Toole, Donal McCann, Niall Toibín, Marie Keane, and Mary O'Hara. Thereafter there were concerts in Ireland, television and radio work in England, and trips to Brittany, Belgium, and the Netherlands. Come April and it was back to North America for another coast-to-coast tour and their first appearance in Carnegie Hall.

By this stage the band had been operating on a full-time basis for only eight months, but the pattern for the future had been moulded. The show was without question on the road.

6 Seán

Back in the days when the Chieftains were still in the process of building their reputation, the present writer chanced to be driving through a rather rugged part of County Wicklow shortly after a snow blizzard. Suddenly he noticed a huge man at the top of a pole, engaged in repairing a fallen line, and thought to himself, 'That must be the tallest telephone engineer in Ireland.' The thought may well have been quite accurate. However the same man is also perhaps the tallest fiddler in Ireland, and one of the best. His name is Seán Keane.

The most ardent upholder of traditional values would agree that Seán's credentials as a folk musician are impeccable. Each of his parents came from an area in Ireland where the music has survived as a rich regional heritage, and each passed on to him this legacy. His mother originated in County Longford in the North Midlands, and his father came from Clare. Countless townlands and villages in that county have given their names as the titles of dance tunes so it is hardly surprising that a piece prominent in Seán's personal repertoire is the 'Ballynacally Reel', for here his father was reared.

Seán was fortunate to enjoy the best of both schools of musical education. In the home the folk tradition was all around and was assimilated as naturally as learning to walk. But formal training was also regarded as important and when a child he was entered in the Dublin School of Music. As a soloist he has been rated amongst the top few fiddlers in Ireland for many years now but yet has never ceased to be a student of his instrument. He has always remained fascinated by the technique and style of other musicians — pipers as well as fiddlers, indeed a great affinity to the playing of Willie Clancy is particularly apparent in his first solo album *Gusty's Frolics*.

Seán Keane has been totally at home on the fiddle since the age of six. Often prodigies fail to live up to early promise, but in his case the inherent natural talent has flourished with the added component of experience. A combination of individuality, respect for tradition, precision, grace, and at times even abandon marks him out as a 'master' fiddler: a proud title but one which he bears easily. He would have made his name as a soloist internationally had he never joined the Chieftains, indeed had he taken a totally different musical direction he would have been equipped to hold his own amongst the best of the jazz fiddlers. For all that, he is well able to blend in as a member of the team.

Seán and his wife Marie have three children. She is a native of County Clare, raised in the town of Ennistymon. Seán has always shown a great commitment to young people for he is one of nature's born teachers. Many a young musician has had cause to be thankful for his influence and advice. It is a moving sight to witness this giant of a man clutching his instrument and bow and surrounded by a group of fledgling fiddlers. Nor has the pace of life with the Chieftains dulled this enthusiasm for passing on the tradition he inherited to the musicians of the future.

7 *Westward the Chieftains*

The North American continent has played a generous and crucial role in the development of the Chieftains' international image, especially since the band embarked on a full-time career. From their earliest tours to the United States and Canada the people took them to their hearts, and for their part the members of the group have returned there again and again, sometimes as often as three times or more in a single year.

There is no question that being Irish helps: at the same time it has never been the policy to play up the shamrock and shillelagh image. The Chieftains have proved themselves popular with ethnic groups from Nova Scotia to California, from Vancouver to Florida, as well as most places in between. They have known the experience of playing in New Mexico before an audience largely comprised of admirers drawn from the Indian and Hispanic communities, many of whom had travelled hundreds of miles to be there. The local promoter mentioned that it was the biggest crowd which he had attracted that season.

Of course North America dictates its own pace, exhausting by European standards but also exhilarating; yet necessary for success in that part of the world and now an accepted aspect of the Chieftains' working lives. It is a world in which good publicists such as Charlie Comer play an essential role. During a promotional 'recce' in the Spring of 1983, Paddy reckons that Charlie arranged for him no fewer than twenty-eight interviews in a single day.

Some idea of the pressures of touring can be gauged from a glance at the work diary for March 25, the previous year. The band embarked at 6 a.m. to fly to Minneapolis from their last venue. On arrival in that city they were due at a television studio at 12 noon. One hour later they were dashing to another studio to take part in the daily womens' programme. Later, on arrival back at their hotel there was a further film crew waiting for them, and at 5 p.m. two more TV teams turned up at their sound check in the concert hall. That was five television appearances behind them and a live performance to come — just one day in a twenty-two day tour during which they enjoyed precisely three free evenings. The irony was that the show had been well sold out long before all this hectic promotional activity took place.

With their professional life so dominated by tight travel schedules, the Chieftains have managed to honour their

CHUCK PULIN

engagements very successfully. Once, admittedly, they were almost two hours late for a concert in Salt Lake City due to a delayed flight connection from Seattle. It wasn't a good omen for no one was overly confident as to how they would be received in the Mormon capital. As it turned out the crowd waited patiently and gave them one of their most memorable receptions. Afterwards there was a splendid meal and even a drop of the hard stuff, a surprising bonus allowing for the mores of that community. On a subsequent visit to the same city, Paddy had an unusual confrontation when, after a concert, he was approached by an elderly lady anxious to hold his hands to acquire some of this 'charismatic' energy which she had observed during the show.

Civic honour is a traditional American way of extending friendship to well-known visiting artists. Keys of the city have been bestowed on the Chieftains by the Mayor of Boston as well as the late Edward Daly of Chicago. Similar welcomes were accorded by Jersey City, Rochester, Springfield, Worcester, and Schenectady, while during a 1985 tour the group was granted the 'Freedom of the City' of New Bedford. It was reported that the local police department felt it necessary to warn Derek that the privilege did not include encouraging him to wander in parts of the town where he might get mugged.

Just before their first visit to Detroit, during a radio interview Paddy joked that perhaps the mayor of the auto capital of the world might consider honouring him with a new car. The dignitary in question, by name of O'Katz (he added the O for the occasion), attended a press conference to deliver a speech of welcome. He mentioned that he had heard that Mr Moloney would like to return home with an automobile, 'which I've got for him right here'. His honour proceeded to present him with the latest proto-type — but dangling from the end of a key-ring!

Again considering the pace of North American trips, the Chieftains have been reasonably lucky with regard to illness. There have been times when individual members of the band have dragged themselves on stage dying from the 'flu, but not too frequently. Once Paddy took a nasty fall at a reception in the Irish Pavilion in New York. Largely his own fault, for he had been attempting to assist Carmel Quinn bodily over a rope barrier, ignoring that the singer was more generously proportioned than he. A nagging pain resulted which grew excruciating when next he buckled on the pipes. Later in the tour a consultation with a Californian doctor diagnosed a cracked rib, which when bound up made the process of pipering considerably less painful.

Most musicians who have been on the road can tell hair-raising tales about some of the establishments laying claim to the status of

Paddy with 'Tip' O'Neill, Edward Kennedy and others at the Capitol Building, Washington DC

65

'theatrical digs'. This no doubt is one reason why the Chieftains make it a rule to stop over in comfortable hotels during extended tours, certainly since success has accompanied their trail. It did however prove a new experience in luxury to rest their weary heads at l'Hermitage in Hollywood on more than one occasion.

Their patronising this extraordinary concept in inn-keeping (where the walls are covered in art masterpieces) results from special arrangements between the band and the proprietors. The Chieftains agree to play a short concert before invited guests, and in return each member has the privilege of living it up in a personal suite which in the normal course of events would cost several hundred dollars per night. In addition the hotel has proved a valuable oasis for making contact with the film world. It was at l'Hermitage that Paddy met the documentary director Miriam Birch which directly led to his writing the score for *The Ballad of the Irish Horse*, commissioned by the National Geographic Society, which in turn subsequently led to the release of an album. Here too he discussed with Ron Howard, then enjoying his success as the director of *Splash*, the probabilities of composing further scores. And it was also at l'Hermitage that Paddy became acquainted with John Travolta.

Paddy contrasts the luxury of the hotel with other examples of accommodation which the band experienced earlier in its career. The most stark, not to say dramatic, was on the island of Groix off the coast of Brittany. During their first visit to the Lorient Festival they had agreed to play at an elaborate birthday party at a club on the island, only to find that the sleeping quarters were confined to a war-time bunker: a bomb shelter with iron bars on the door and beds so damp that it was necessary to cover them with plastic sheeting. Still, the party had gone well and all slept soundly. Next morning the organiser of it all woke the Chieftains by way of singing extracts from Handel's Harp Concerto!

It is perhaps surprising that the group had experienced many an American tour before first visiting Texas in 1981. They have since returned on numerous occasions, for the Lone Star state lived up to its reputation. Paddy describes it as 'absolute magic' and as being 'a world on its own'. What he means is a part of the continent where the hospitality is lavish, the music alive, and the audiences warm and uninhibited, be they in Austin, Houston, San Antonio, or Corpus Christi.

The first trip was organised by Chessley Millikan, an Irishman with a big reputation in the promotional field in America who has managed artists of the calibre of the Grateful Dead. Indirectly he was responsible for the Chieftains taking up the challenge of grass-roots American traditional music in the form of 'Cotton Eyed Joe'. Chessley chanced to play the tune on cassette while he and the band were motoring in the direction of Willie Nelson's Oprey House. The number was an old American country favourite, but

On the set of the Today *show, NBC studios, New York, March 1986*

Paddy recognised it as a version of the Irish reel 'The Mountain Top', or if you will 'O I can wash my Daddy's Shirt, O I can wash it clean'. He was hardly out of the car before he ran up an arrangement for fun. But the fun caught on, and before long 'Cotton Eyed Joe' was released as a single as well as on an album, an extra touch of authenticity being added by Derek tinkling a genuine honky-tonk piano.

Despite the excitement of trips to the United States in the company of his fellow musicians, one of Paddy's fondest memories is of touring America on the lecture circuit. This took place about two years before the band turned full-time and was organised by Eoin McKiernan of the Irish-American Cultural Institute. It was a journey of contrast which at one point found Rita and himself hosted by the O'Shaughnessys of St Paul, an American-Irish dynasty noted for patronising the arts.

Much of the time Paddy was in the company of students for the tour included a number of colleges. He was surprised and pleased to find that they showed as much interest in the lore surrounding the music as they did to his illustrations on whistle and pipes. He has one especially pleasant memory of a group of young people listening spellbound while he told the tale of how Seán Aerach Ó Seanacháin had learnt the air 'An Buachaill Caol Dubh' in a dream while asleep in a fairy fort. Seán Aerach had been tutor to an eighteenth-century Knight of Glin, and Paddy had first heard the story from the present Knight, Desmond FitzGerald, on a guided tour during one of his visits to Glin Castle.

The lecture tour had its lighter moments as when Paddy struck up the pipes having first insisted that Rita, much to her mortification, lead about three hundred assembled students through 'The Siege of Ennis'. The trip had taken place during the height of the streaking season and on one occasion a young man in Massachusetts, totally starkers, was apprehended at the point of entering the auditorium. The organisers were relieved that he failed to gain admission to the lecture, although the lecturer himself had other ideas: 'It would have added a great bit of life to the proceedings.'

In the United States, as elsewhere, success or failure is essentially determined by the attitude of audiences. Nevertheless the fact that the Chieftains have attracted the attention of many people prominent in the world of showbusiness has certainly not inhibited their popularity as visiting artists. Often such contacts have been made through social events. On one occasion they attended a party given for them by Leonard Rosenman, composer of many film scores such as *East of Eden*. The company included the actor Burgess Meredith who has since proved a staunch friend to the group whenever it plays on the West Coast. Also present was Carroll O'Connor, star of *All in the Family* and an actor with long-standing Dublin connections, having worked for a period with the

Paddy with Jackson Browne at the Lisdoonvarna Festival, 1982

Gate Theatre. Another Chieftains fan is the world's favourite 'baddy', Larry Hagman alias JR. Paddy spent one hilarious evening trying to make off with his ten-gallon hat.

Contacts in the more strictly musical field have ranged from Henry Mancini to The Band. Dan Fogelberg might not be immediately associated with Irish traditional music and yet he invited the Chieftains to provide an item on one of his albums. Paddy and Derek did likewise for the popular country rock singer Don Henley, leader of The Eagles. Henley in fact was so concerned about the transportation of Derek's instruments that he provided a magnificent set of boxes at his own expense.

During one American tour, Art Garfunkel turned up at a

The Carnegie Hall, New York has been the scene of many triumphant concerts.

concert in Buffalo to ask the Chieftains to record for him on a forth-coming album. This wasn't possible at the time because of the schedule, however at a later stage he was prepared to travel to Dublin to do the job which was engineered at Lombard Studios. He stayed in a suite at the Shelbourne Hotel and was entertained at some of the best restaurants, which must have appealed to him for he remained much longer than he had planned, and eventually sent over a golden disc in recognition of the Chieftains' contribution.

Jackson Browne is yet another popular American singer to frequent Chieftains' concerts and he and Paddy got together at the Lisdoonvarna Festival. Later Paddy joined him for four concerts at the London Odeon to accompany precisely one song. It was 'The Crow in the Cradle', a powerful indictment of nuclear insanity. In more recent times, Paddy added instrumental colour to a three-lady album featuring the combined talents of Dolly Parton, Emmylou Harris, and Linda Ronstadt.

Although the Chieftains would see themselves essentially as live concert artists, they have also always had the knack of using the media to advantage. In America, television in particular has brought them before enormous audiences through shows such as *US Today* or Father Peyton's *Great Mysteries* which was introduced by the late Princess Grace and filmed at Dublin Castle. At a different level Paddy has arranged music for Public Service Broad-casting, in particular for an award-nominated television version of *The Playboy of the Western World* directed by Vincent Dowling, formerly of the Abbey. But in relation to mass audiences, an important occasion was a ten-minute spot by the band on the *Today* show in 1986 as this programme currently rides the top of the United States television ratings.

It would be difficult to estimate which particular television performance has been most influential for the group, although an appearance on *Saturday Night Live* must rate highly. The show had an estimated fifty-two million viewers and was superbly produced. During rehearsals there was an attempt to introduce an element of stage-Irishness but this was successfully resisted. This series is something of an institution and past highlights are still repeated.

An incident before the programme surprised the musicians as to the type of underhand pressures which are brought to bear on artists appearing in such mass-media productions. Despite security, the local distributor of a new brand of whiskey managed to deposit a crate of his product in the dressing room, along with an implied suggestion that he would be more than generous should a bottle of the stuff find its way onto the set during transmission.

It was not the first time that Paddy had been subjected to this rather seamy aspect of show business. Once, after checking into an American hotel, he was contacted by an attractive redhead who just happened to have reserved the room next door. She invited him to step in and discuss a business proposition, and once again

Paddy and Mick Jagger at Right Track Studios, New York, recording for Mick's solo album, March 1987

the product marketed by her principals was alcoholic. At the arranged time he was astounded to find that her room was furnished with a degree of extravagant luxury not apparent elsewhere in the building, and including a very obviously placed antique double bed. The lady, who was scantily clad, suggested that for a start he might allow her to photograph him standing beside a pyramidical display of bottles of the booze in question. He had no doubt that she had some further suggestions to pass the time after the camera session. Realising that he had been set up he departed — leaving no doubt as to his feelings.

Almost without exception, the printed media in the States has treated the band with warmth and even impish humour. In February 1986 Todd Everett, staff writer on the Los Angeles *Herald Examiner*, declared: 'If voices had color Paddy Moloney's would be green. Such professional Hollywood Irishmen as Pat O'Brien and Dennis Day would envy his accent and the Irish descended present occupant of the White House only slightly beats him in the gift o'gab department. When Paddy Moloney's on the phone from Dublin the atmosphere's so thick you can almost hear the shamrocks growing in the background.'

In their earlier careers as individual musicians, each of the Chieftains had a wealth of experience playing in a variety of venues, everything from village halls hardly equipped to exclude the winds of winter let alone provide an adequate acoustic. But from the formation of the band the suitability of venue has always been an important consideration.

Since their first North American tour the group has played in some of the most celebrated concert halls on the continent. It has appeared as guests of the Baltimore Symphony Orchestra, and played in the Chicago Opera House, the O'Shaughnessy Auditorium in St Paul, Madison Square Garden, the Massey Hall in Toronto, the Amazon Theatre in Los Angeles, and Boston Symphony Hall. To most European artists the ambition to make even one appearance in Carnegie Hall can be a lifetime's pipe-dream. The Chieftains have played there so often that Paddy regards the building with an almost cavalier attitude: 'You get to like the place quite well.'

From time to time they have made appearances in auditoriums which are in themselves interesting because of adventurous design or construction. The Mechanics' Hall in Worcester, Massachusetts, is in every sense a modern concert hall but built within the shell of an historic building originally used by craftsmen as their association rooms. In contrast, the building housing the Music Fair in Westbury, New York is entirely contemporary. The stage actually revolves during performances, completing a full circle every forty-five minutes.

For the musician seeking culinary delights the Roy Thompson Hall in Toronto takes some beating. The auditorium has the back-

Seán Keane

up of an elaborate kitchen where gourmet fare is prepared for artists. With champagne flowing after their sound check, the Chieftains found it a sore temptation to break their strict rule of avoiding all excesses prior to performance. When they played there the hall was relatively new, and not long before their friend James Galway had found cause for complaint due to the excessive draught on stage. Paddy concedes that he had a point but has only praise for the management of the establishment and indeed the acoustics.

Audiences do not always realise that the ability to play in a relaxed and seemingly effortless manner is a measure of professionalism rather than a happy act of God. An easy shortcut to relaxation is with the help of alcohol but this inevitably tends to have an ill effect on musical performance, which is why the members of the band stick to their rule of moderation. Before a concert spirits, for instance, are out.

There are some things of course which can rattle musicians during performance. Just prior to a concert in Boston, Seán Potts mislaid his favourite whistle, and although he had a perfectly adequate replacement the loss of the instrument upset him considerably. During the first half his concern had a domino reaction on the others. Happily in the interval the whistle was discovered, safely in the guts of a grand piano where it had rolled, and Seán reverted to his customary ebullience. Paddy too lost a favourite whistle, stolen by a dressing room 'well-wisher' after the show. It was all the more upsetting for it had previously gone missing for a decade, emerging from under a ton of fuel in the coal hole where his son Aonghus, then a toddler, had deposited it.

The format of Chieftains' concerts is by no means totally standardised, for since the first tours new ideas and features have constantly been introduced. The special Christmas show has now become a regular date every other year on the American itinerary. At these events the band is joined by troupes of strawboys and a host of special guests such as James Galway, Geraldine Fitzgerald, Milo O'Shea, Siobhán McKenna, Carmel Quinn, and in 1985 Burgess Meredith. Domestically this can prove a risky business, as it means that usually they make it home across the Atlantic only just about in time to carve the turkey.

Naturally such an emphasis on touring as far off as North America has its worrying aspects for there are families at home trying to live a normal life. To ease this element of domestic stress the group decided to try out the experiment of taking working holidays. The band's schedule is planned around a particular spot where the families stay over on extended vacations. It works well. Cape Cod is one place which has proved a suitable centre for this operation although one might wonder how much of the time is actually given over to R&R. While holidaying there in July 1982 for instance the band also toured Texas, visited the Milwaukee

Festival and the Knoxville World's Fair, and went on location for a large proportion of their Guinness television commercial. But for the Moloneys in particular Cape Cod has proved a relaxing place where they stay with close family friends, the Davitts. Jack Davitt is a grandnephew of Michael Davitt, founder of the Irish Land League.

Recent North American tours have incorporated a successful exercise in community involvement in which local pipe bands and step dancers have directly taken part in the Chieftains' programmes. This has created great interest in cities such as Windsor, Milwaukee, Madison, Denver, Seattle, and Los Angeles as well as other communities in California, Utah, and Kansas.

Of late dancing has become an important aspect of concerts, with the world step-dancing champion, Michael Flatley of Chicago, a regular guest. Much of the Chieftains' material began as accompaniment to the dance and it is interesting that through the development of their concert routine there has been a return to the original function of the music. It also adds visual enrichment to stage performances.

A further development in the group's commitment to the art of dancing took place during their 1986 tour when, in cooperation with the Patricia Coleman Dance Ensemble, Paddy arranged music for 'Ellis Landing', a celebration through modern dance of the Irish emigrant saga. It was originally performed at UCLA, and later the Kennedy Center, with the University of Dayton, Ohio, eventually paying for the transportation of the entire company and the musicians to perform there.

A world champion Irish dancer is one thing, but a guest artist who happens to be a leading Chinese instrumentalist is quite another. Yet the famous *erhu* virtuoso, Chen Hsi-Chuan, has indeed toured with the band including a thirty-eight city itinerary in 1985. Each night he played a ten-minute solo spot, but also joined the rest for a rendition of the old Irish harp composition 'Tabhair Dom de Lámh'.

When the tour commenced in Los Angeles, Chen had been studying English for no more than six months. Nevertheless he gallantly allowed himself to be interviewed on the coast-to-coast TV show *Entertainment Tonight*. There he offered his own description of the typical way in which a Chieftains' concert winds up: 'When Mr Chief signs off says "Oiche Mhait, Slán, Bye Bye, See you all again", and then adds for his own amusement "Up the Yard!"'

During that particular tour in Los Angeles the Chieftains played the three film suites, *Tristan and Isolde, The Year of the French* and *The Ballad of an Irish Horse,* along with full orchestra. The previous year they performed two of these works with the Milwaukee Symphony Orchestra. This had demanded painstaking preparation, for although Paddy had arranged the suites for chamber and concert

The Chieftains were the first group ever to give a concert at the Capitol Building, Washington DC. Here they are in the Sam Rayburn room.

orchestras it was quite another task to adapt the score to accommodate eighty pieces. But worth it: 'The sound was mighty.' It is planned to repeat the Milwaukee concert in 1987.

One of their many tours of Canada was marked by a parliamentary lunch at the invitation of the Prime Minister. As the members of the band approached the House of Commons, they noticed a group demonstrating on behalf of Indian rights outside the House. After ringing the bell Paddy announced themselves as 'The Chieftains' to the attendant, who rather rudely left them on the step while he went to find more information from one of the members within. This procedure was repeated no less than three times, at which point Paddy became positively irate. 'We're the Chieftains from Ireland, officially invited here for lunch.' At last the penny dropped. The doorman had assumed that they were part of the demonstration.

With all their many experiences in America, it would be difficult to single out one particular incident as having paramount importance. There is however a unique aspect to the Chieftains' appearance in the Capitol Building in Washington, DC. This took place during one of their 1983 tours, when they were invited to give a recital as part of the ceremonies marking the inauguration of a scholarship to Boston College sponsored by the Guinness Corporation. In the course of the day they were to meet and have long discussions with prominent Irish American politicians such as Tip O'Neill and Ted Kennedy. All unusual, but why so unique? In fact no other musical group had ever been invited to play there in the history of the United States.

8 Derek

'I don't belong to this century.'

The statement remained unchallenged by the compère of an afternoon radio programme in the Summer of 1985. Given the twentieth-century obsession with packaging human talents in neat parcels, the speaker — Derek Bell — was quite right. It would be well nigh impossible to pigeon-hole his particular talents. Creatively, he is indeed more like a child of the Renaissance.

Derek is the Chieftains' only Ulsterman and he and his wife Stefanie still make their home in Belfast, although she originally came from the United States. He has always been a musician, virtually since infancy. At that stage of his life his parents were

Derek Bell

advised that by the age of two he would suffer serious visual impairment and at once started to compensate for this by surrounding him with playthings which appealed to the ear. Happily the medical prognosis proved inaccurate, although this parental concern resulted in Derek developing an amazingly acute ear as well as an early aptitude for music. At the age of twleve he composed a piano concerto.

When Derek resigned from the Northern Ireland BBC Orchestra to join the band he already had a brilliant musical career behind him. His education took him to the Royal College of Music in London as well as further afield to study under Leon Goosens and Madame Rosina Lhevine in Colorado. The latter he once described as a remarkable woman who combined the virtues of 'love, wisdom, and discipline'. However he would also acknowledge the late David Curry of the BBC in Belfast as a major influence on his development.

Nowadays the public would generally associate Derek with the harp, yet initially his primary instruments were in the keyboard range. As time went on he turned his attention to the oboe, cor anglais, and dulcimer; and after joining the Chieftains a long interest in the psaltery family led to his reconstruction of the ancient Irish timpan. At one period of his life he was principal oboe, horn, and piano player with the American Wind Symphony Orchestra. As a soloist he has appeared with the Royal Philharmonic Orchestra as well as the Pittsburgh, Moscow, Budapest, and London Symphony Orchestras and has no less than five solo albums to his credit, four on harp and one on piano.

Once when Derek was passing through Moscow airport en route to fulfil an engagement, he caused considerable consternation amongst the security guards who had cause to believe that he had been wired up to explode due to a mysterious sound of ticking. There was an explanation. Before leaving home he had grabbed a full-sized alarm clock and stuffed it in his jacket pocket along with various bits and pieces of musical paraphernalia. Derek's friends, who have been known to refer to him as 'Ding Dong Bell' (a name irreverently bestowed on him by Paddy during a live performance), would claim this story as typical of the man. He has never found the slightest difficulty in adapting to a career based on traditional music. He believes passionately that there is much more in common between the various branches of music than that which divides them.

9 The Chieftains Abroad

To emphasise the part that North America has played in the lives of the Chieftains in no way takes from their role as musical globe-trotters elsewhere in the world. That portion of the earth's surface which they have as yet to visit is rapidly becoming an ever-diminishing territory. One can forecast with confidence that between the time of writing and the publication of this book new countries will have been added to the itinerary. Often it has been their privilege to open up fresh fields for other Irish musicians to follow on.

It might be assumed that there is considerable variation in the reaction of different audiences in widely scattered geographic locations. Surprisingly this is not the case: the band attracts a similar enthusiam whether playing at home, in Scandinavia, Germany, Austria, the Netherlands, Greece, Iceland, Belgium, Switzerland, Spain, or even Hong Kong. To comment that music

The Chieftains and a chieftain at Dublin Airport

transcends all linguistic barriers must amount to the most classic of clichés, but it is an apt enough appraisal of what in fact happens. One is forced to admit the justice of Paddy's recurring philosophy: *the music speaks for itself.*

Irish people have sometimes referred to Great Britain as 'the old enemy'. Whatever about the political and historic reasons for the stormy relations between the neighbouring islands, the Chieftains have always found that British audiences are second to none in their welcome. It might be thought that the large Irish presence in England can explain why the band is able to pack venues such as the Royal Albert and Festival Halls, but this is not the explanation. It would stretch credibility to suggest that the Irish alone were mobilised to elect the Chieftains top of the *Melody Maker* poll. The group indeed plays Irish music, but, as in North America, has always avoided flaunting the stage-Irish image 'across the water', and has proved equally successful in areas of Britain where there is no obvious Irish emigrant population.

The appeal of the Chieftains to the British public dates back to the mix-sixties. At that time the folk music business was booming and it was understandable that their dynamic approach to the music should have attracted a vigorous following among the thousands of folk fans. Yet contrary to general trends this following has been sustained, and two decades later is actually stronger than ever.

Paddy has always been careful not to take support for the group in Britain for granted. Keeping the momentum going has resulted in a lot of work in terms of publicity and in the arranging of carefully plotted tours. In 1980 for instance there were grounds to suspect that the drawing power of the Chieftains was beginning to ebb. His reaction was to take the bull by the horns and organise a punishing three-week twenty-concert tour covering not only the Royal Albert Hall and venues in the larger cities of Manchester, Birmingham, Edinburgh, and Bristol but also places such as Southport, Maesteg, Derby, and Brighton. There was even a performance in the Royal Shakespeare Theatre in Stratford-on-Avon. The policy of showing the flag with a vengeance proved effective and at the end of the three weeks there was no doubt as to their popularity in England, Scotland, and Wales.

That particular tour had added importance, for all the concerts in the London area were associated with the Sense of Ireland Festival. This ambitious showcase brought to the British capital every aspect of creative endeavour in Ireland and it was only right that the Chieftains and a host of other musicians and singers should have presented traditional music as a vital aspect of that side of Irish life. Not long afterwards the band was back in London for the

With the Boomtown Rats in Sydney, Australia; Bob Geldof (centre)

83

*Only a reflection of himself
- Derek Bell in Minnesota*

British premiere of *Playboy* with the Irish Ballet Company. In this rather different context, their success may be judged by Sadler's Wells being sold out every night of the run.

Some three years previously Paddy had arranged on tape incidental music for a straight version of that play staged by the National Theatre in London. To mark the end of eighteen months' continuous performance the Chieftains were asked to play a concert in the theatre itself. It was a concert with a difference for they actually did the show from the stage as set up for the play, drops, props, and all. Of course the less confined atmosphere of a folk festival is a more typical environment for the band. They have

Unaccustomed garb! A promotional picture for the Breton album released in 1987

On tour in China, 1984

TERRY LOTT

played many of these over the years, and in the case of the big Cambridge Festival returned in 1981 after a twelve-year absence to share the bill with Donovan. In the ensuing period there have been two further appearances at the Festival.

Rock festivals have also appeared on the itinerary — an indication that those who attend such events are musically more broad minded than given credit. For the Chieftains the Crystal Palace 'Garden Party' was a welcome excursion into this realm of British musical life, as it provided them with the relief of an open air arena in the middle of a lengthy series of studio sessions. The festival centred around the brilliant guitarist Eric Clapton, and it

Derek and CBS ex-president Maurice (Obie) Oberstein

87

*Derek beside Oisín
Kelly's last sculpture, the
blind harper O'Carolan*

was he who invited them to play a set during his own concert.

British radio and television have featured the Chieftains on all manner of programmes from *The Old Grey Whistle Test* to *Lucky Numbers*. On occasion they have shared the bill with musicians far removed from the traditional sphere. Oscar Peterson, the world famous Canadian jazz pianist, appeared on a programme which they made in London, but to Paddy's everlasting regret lack of rehearsal time prevented a joint performance. On other shows Russell Harty actually danced to their music — much to the amazement of his public — and Val Doonican joined them playing the bodhrán. Truth to tell, Kevin Conneff had travelled over ahead in order to tutor him.

One media experience which especially excited Paddy was their appearance on the BBC programme *Sight and Sound*. He went so far as to describe it as 'our most prestigious broadcast to date'. Television and radio were simultaneously linked up, so the dedicated viewer had the option of enjoying a perfectly balanced stereo transmission. The items played by the band included a full-length fifteen-minute performance of the piece 'Bonaparte's Retreat'.

There was an unusual, even bizarre, follow up to a conversation between Paddy and Gloria Hunniford on her BBC World Service chat and disc show. Sometime after the broadcast Gloria received a letter requesting more information about the Chieftains and their records. It came from a British family living abroad who hadn't been able to devote as much attention to the programme as they would have wished. This was due to their having listened to it while crouching under the dining room table. There they had taken refuge, for the city where they resided was in a state of siege with bullets and shrapnel flying liberally through the air. Later when Gloria told him about the letter, Moloney was heard to comment, 'We get to people in the strangest places.'

From earliest times there has been close musical contact between Ireland and Scotland. Paddy was struck by many of the similarities when he went to Orkney to record the poet George Mackay Brown for Claddagh and took the opportunity to enjoy the vivacity of island fiddling. Scots and Scots-Gaelic poetry was a speciality of the Claddagh spoken arts catalogue so he visited that country frequently, cultivating deep friendships with poets such as Somhairle Mac Ghill-Eain and Hugh Mac Diarmid who recorded two albums of verse.

These trips also opened up many musical contacts and as a result the Chieftains are well known to Scottish audiences through tours, radio and television, and numerous performances at the Edinburgh Festival. It was at the 1978 Festival that they appeared as guests of Van Morrison. To close the show, 'Van the Man' and the band played a joint set before an audience of several thousand.

Two of the lengthier pieces regularly played by the Chieftains,

'Bonaparte's Retreat' and 'The Year of the French', emphasise through Moloney's composition the long historical links between Ireland and France. In the second half of the twentieth century these links have been fortified by constant exchange visits by both amateur and professional musicians from the two countries. Unquestionably, Irish music has become a permanent feature of the French folk scene with French groups, such as Shamrock, specialising in it. There is a French branch of Comhaltas Ceoltóirí Éireann, as well as the Centre de Musique Irlandaise at Montigny, while the popular magazine *Tradition Vivante* often carries articles and interviews of Irish interest.

The Chieftains would find it hard to recollect just how often they have visited France. They have played in every part of the country but have an especially strong association with the Celtic province of Brittany. The annual Lorient Festival could almost be termed a mandatory engagement in a given year, and there the musicians have also spent pleasant working vacations with their families.

At Lorient 1983 the group performed two of the film suites with the Festival Orchestra under the baton of James Morreau and also recruited three excellent local pipers to play the 'Irish March' from *The Year of the French*. The press in France raved about the show although at an early stage of the evening disaster threatened. The whole event had been planned to take place in the open air, but a sudden deluge of rain forced the organisers to switch venue to the Palais de Congrès. As Paddy remembers, 'They packed two and a half thousand people into a sixteen hundred seater. They were hanging from the rafters, but it was terrific.'

Since the fifties, Brittany has had a personal appeal for Paddy, for there he disembarked on his first ever trip abroad, travelling by way of Fokker Friendship aircraft. He was bound for the Celtic Congress, pipes in hand, and the experience opened up a new world for him. He stayed with a big friendly farmer and still remembers his wife's 'home-made bread and apricot jam for breakfast'.

Vivid memories of that first visit to Brittany have remained with him: the extraordinary local interest in Irish music and all things Irish, the compère at a concert referring to his 'oolin' pipes, the colour and the style of the dancers, and operating his box Brownie to photograph a young teenager playing the Breton biniou by the name of Alan Stivell. Many return trips with the Chieftains have reinforced those early happy impressions. In all sorts of ways Brittany seems very close to home, and over the years he has maintained a close professional and friendly relationship with Polig Montjarret, the famous Breton musician and collector.

Galicia in Northern Spain is another area in Europe with a

Paddy on a promotional tour for The Chieftains' first concert at the Albert Hall in March 1975

Celtic heritage, especially in the musical field. When the Irish academic musician Professor Walter Starkie visited the province as a young man, long before the days of developed mass communications, he brought along his fiddle to play the jigs and the reels to local people. In fact they thought he was playing Galician music, so similar are the styles.

It is an area where the Chieftains found a deep response to their music. When they played under the sky at Vigo, the audience lit candles as darkness fell, creating a beautiful atmosphere. Later the Galician group Milladorio, which includes an uilleann piper, came to record an album in Dublin. The piper ran into difficulties with his reed and rang Paddy for help. This he rendered, even contributing a passage on the disc for which he was rewarded with a bottle of their rough local spirit.

Italy has also proved a happy hunting ground for the group. This is itself again emphasises the curious appeal of the Chieftains, for in general there has never been obvious Italian participation in the international comings and goings of folk musicians. The audiences there are usually very young and the curtain tends to rise a couple of hours behind schedule, yet there is no denying the joy of the response.

On one Italian tour the band played before the Pope, in fact not long after they had participated in the papal mass in Dublin. They entered the pontifical audience room in a state of disarray, needing a change of clothes, and lacking the lick of a razor. They had whiled away the previous hours by playing poker on a night train from Turin and arrived in Rome to find a massive traffic snarl-up which forced them to proceed directly to the Vatican from the station.

The Pope listened to their music and referred to it with pleasure before the large audience during his general address, a copy of which now hangs in the Moloney household. He talked to every member of the group and presented each with a string of rosary beads.

Italy too has personal memories for the Moloneys. In 1981 Rita accompanied Paddy to Venice where he took part in a Eurovision concert with the pop group Albania. They left that beautiful city in torrential rain and Paddy's pipes almost drowned in the canal when he hastily slung them on board a water taxi. The pipes survived the storm, which is more than can be said for Rita's shoes. Some hours later she was perforce barefoot as Italian friends introduced her to the grandeur of Rome.

The first visit of the Chieftains to Greece took place in 1985, and as usual their programme included arrangements of local traditional melodies. During the trip friends drove Paddy to the 4th century BC theatre at Epidauros where he was prevailed on to test the famous acoustic. He played a number of tunes on the whistle from a particular spot and sure enough it was reported back

Paddy with record chiefs Garech a Brún, Claddagh, and Maurice (Obie) Oberstein, ex CBS

to him that he could be clearly heard all over the auditorium which seats fourteen thousand. More than that, groups of unforeseen tourists greeted the impromptu recital with applause.

The ancient theatre is still used for an annual drama festival and Paddy has since resolved that he would love to play a full concert in these dramatic surroundings. Perhaps it is something which may eventually come to pass, for in the course of the visit to Greece he struck up a cordial relationship with the Minister for Culture, Melina Mercouri.

Although much further away, the Antipodes too has always been friendly territory. When the Chieftains toured New Zealand they were entranced by the beauty of the countryside and the warmth of the people. It was there that they took part in the *Telethon* television spectacular. This was a marathon charity show in which money was raised with the assistance of show business personalities from all over the world, including some of the cast of *Coronation Street*.

On 12 June 1976 the band set off on its first trip to Australia. Up to that date this was their most distant port of call and during the tour there were moments of loneliness. Paddy reckons that he must have been operating on some extrasensory line of communication, for he continually found himself gazing into baby shops in the bigger towns. He wasn't at all surprised when he rang home to hear from Rita that their youngest son Pádraig was on the way. But Australia offered plenty of hectic diversion to dispel feelings of homesickness. As he remembers, 'They went berserk, laying on pipe bands, dancers, and local musicians. Often we were greeted at the airports by TV crews to wind up on the evening news.'

In Sydney the band was based at the Sebel Town House. On a subsequent visit to this hotel they helped Michael Parkinson celebrate his birthday, and the Yorkshireman reciprocated by introducing on Australian television a re-run of programmes featuring their music which he had originally made with the BBC. In Melbourne they were booked to play one concert, but actually did four. Melbourne is a high spot in terms of popularity. The following year total attendances almost reached the fifteen thousand mark.

From time to time the band has also played away from the larger population centres. Mount Isa in North Queensland was an interesting community made up largely of miners, many of whom were of Irish background. Before doing a promo, Paddy was surprised to find himself escorted to an *outdoor* waiting room at the television station. In the surrounding countryside the soil was red in colour, and the whole atmosphere reminded the band of a western movie set. Martin Fay went so far as to claim that with his own two eyes he had seen John Wayne ride into town.

Australia has a family interest for Paddy for it is there that his great-grandfather emigrated, marrying a girl from back home. The couple actually decided to return to Ireland for the birth of their first child but tragically she died on arrival in Liverpool shortly after being delivered of a son. The little boy, Paddy's grandfather, was raised in Ireland by relatives but his father returned to Australia where in time·all contact was lost. Paddy's ambition is some day to try and piece together the rest of the story.

In 1983 the Chieftains approached Australia from the direction of Hong Kong in the wake of their China trip. On this occasion they visited Tasmania, where they ran into James Galway for the second time in the course of the tour. It was a good opportunity to start hatching the plot which in time resulted in their joint album. The eventual recording of this was filmed by the BBC as a documentary with the intention of issuing it as a video. The scenario included the aftermath of the sessions in the form of a New Year's party at Paddy's home. He tends to make quite an event of these gatherings, insisting that all guests do their party piece. His neighbour, film maker John Boorman, has never been known to perform elsewhere.

There have been in all many trips to Australia, although one of the most vivid memories is of an incident which arose during the first visit. The weather was roasting and late at night the Chieftains collectively plunged into their hotel pool to cool off after the show. The party included bones player Ronnie McShane who took to the water clad in his underpants. On emerging, he removed these, before making his way through the public quarters of the building, draped in a towel. He hadn't allowed for the guile of Seán Keane who slipped up behind him and whipped away his protective toga. In desperation he flung the wet garment at his assailant and fled for the sanctuary of his room. Next morning when the Chieftains appeared for a communal breakfast, the first thing they noticed was one pair of male knickers hanging from the handle of the dining room door.

94

The historic Liberties of Dublin have always played a special part in the life of Ireland's capital. Despite its situation just south of the river Liffey in the middle of the city, this area is rich in community life. It is a quality which has persisted into the present day even if most of the rest of the inner metropolis has become a place where people no longer live. Kevin Conneff is a Liberties man. Traditional music is usually associated with country areas rather than long standing urban communities. Not so in the Liberties. Here it has been cherished in many households for as long as anyone can remember, and longer. Back indeed to the times of Zozimus, the eighteenth-century ballad monger who sang to the citizens of his day such rich and lasting ballads as 'The Finding of Moses'.

Kevin Conneff

But Kevin came to folk music comparatively late in life, that is at about eighteen years of age. Like many another young person at that time he found in it a dimension of meaning not always apparent in the more commercial music of the day, and it was in his nature to become an active participant rather than an onlooker.

As well as his musical talents Kevin was to bring organisational abilities to the folk scene in which he surrounded himself. In those days there were innumerable 'singing' pubs all over Dublin which attracted large crowds and sold a prodigious amount of beer. In most of these establishments the conditions for singers and musicians were dire, their offerings reduced to little more than background to the boozing. Kevin was one of those to found the Tradition Club, meeting in Slatterys of Capel Street once a week. Here the music reigned supreme, order being maintained yet in a relaxed atmosphere. The place became a mecca for those who really wanted to listen with artists ranging from *sean-nós* singers to well-known international performers.

In the late sixties, along with Christy Moore and others, Kevin featured on the now famous *Prosperous* album which more or less led to the formation of Planxty. As a singer he showed no inclination to follow the fashion of 'crooning' folk-based material. His approach to the old songs in both the Irish and English language has always been in the old style; this he interprets beautifully and usually unaccompanied — the human voice is after all the most ancient of instruments. What must surprise those who would confine this style to the museum is the response he receives in whatever part of the world he happens to perform.

Kevin's singing often demonstrates the power of restraint, but if the mood of the music requires, he can also show restraint on his instrument. This is a rare ability, for many lead musicians have suffered from overly enthusiastic bodhrán batterers: indeed Seamus Ennis was once heard to murmur that the best way to strike a bodhrán was with a penknife. Kevin has keen understanding of the role of the group percussionist, but should the occasion demand he can really make the rhythmic sparks fly. He joined the Chieftains in 1976, appearing with them in public for the first time at the Merriman School in Ennis.

11 The Chieftains at Home

There is an item in the engagement diary on a date in December 1983 which simply reads 'Hollywood'. To jump to the conclusion that this refers to some function in a certain Californian city of cinematographic fame would be erroneous. It records a concert by the Chieftains but the venue is a small village of the same name in west County Wicklow where Kevin Conneff has had long associations. The occasion was a charity performance to raise funds for the renovation of the parish hall.

This rather unextraordinary item somehow encapsulates the spirit and the style of the Chieftains. The venue could easily have been the other Hollywood. The fact that it was a remote community in Ireland tells a great deal about the quality of their commitment, especially when they are 'at home'.

Ireland remains home for all the Chieftains Ireland is where they return after the tensions of the tours and Ireland is where they disperse to wind down, let off steam, and live their own separate lives. Sometimes Ireland is where they also come together, albeit usually in pursuit of their common livelihood.

It was the Irish public who first gave recognition to the Chieftains and in the ensuing years this relationship has been maintained. In between foreign tours considerable attention is paid to the home market — and for solid economic reasons as well as natural sentiment. The band is also generous to local charities, although this is obviously a side to the business which has to be carefully regulated.

The Chieftains have been associated with many of the big events on the Irish festival circuit. During its heyday they were very much in evidence at Lisdoonvarna, and in the capital they have always shown a particular commitment to the Liberties Festival due to their special connections with the city of Dublin. At the 1984 Festival they played their concert in a well-known Liberties landmark, the Church of St Michael and St John on the quays — referred to affectionately by Brendan Behan as 'SS Micky and Jax'.

One of the most extraordinary spectaculars in which the band played its part was the 'Circassia' extravaganza organised by film director Kevin McClory. The affair was in aid of the Central Remedial Clinic in Dublin and mounted at the palatial McClory residence in Straffan, County Kildare. It was one of those rare charitable events in which artists long to partake. As it turned out·

Absorbing the tradition at Garrykennedy, Co. Tipperary

On stage at the twenty-first birthday concert, National Concert Hall, Dublin

the cast list ranged from Shirley MacLaine to Sean Connery and Burgess Meredith. Security was so strict that some of the participants, including the Chieftains and Eric Clapton, found it difficult getting admitted to the premises at all.

The host decided to make a film capturing certain aspects of the night. This contained a sequence in which one P. Moloney, playing the whistle, descended in a hot-air balloon, to be greeted on reaching terra firma by one John Huston. 'God Almighty,' shuddered Paddy on relating the tale, not yet the better of the experience!

Mention of palatial residences is a reminder that it was the Chieftains who opened the now-famous Rolling Stones concert in

Slane Castle in County Meath. 'Slane' has since become almost institutionalised, but in 1982 it was an amazing sight to witness thousands upon thousands of young people making their way from all parts of Ireland, to gather in the castle grounds of this pretty little village on the banks of the river Boyne. They came by car, coach, hot rod, bicycle, and on foot. A few of the more privileged even came by helicopter. For the Chieftains it was the chance to renew old acquaintances. They had hoped to use their set to shoot a sequence for the Guinness commercial, and as it turned out their film crew was the only one which Mick Jagger was prepared to admit. Before the opening Kevin Conneff presented Charlie Watts, the Stones' drummer, with a bodhrán. The gesture sparked off an

The funeral mass for Seán Ó Riada in Coolea, Co. Cork

99

The Pack Horse Bridge.
Paddy and Rita campaigned
successfully to save this bridge
- one of the oldest in Europe
- near their home at
Milltown.

impromptu percussion session, a highlight of the day of which the thousands out front were unaware. For Paddy the occasion was a reminder of previous encounters with the Jaggers. Many years before his son Aonghus, then quite tiny, had beaten Bianca at a game of rings in Keenan's pub in Roundwood. She was far from pleased.

Even hardened professionals might have been forgiven a blast of nerves on walking out before a throng such as had gathered in Slane. But for the Chieftains the crowd was only a fraction of what had been their biggest audience ever. That experience took place on 29 September 1979. That day marked the first visit of a reigning pope to Irish soil.

Early in the morning along with the rest of the crowd the Chieftains made their way to the Phoenix Park hours before the papal mass was due to begin. Like everyone else they were well fortified with packets of sandwiches and flasks of tea. Their first assignment was to play a selection of pieces to warm up the congregation before the arrival of John Paul II. To celebrate the event Paddy had arranged a piece sometimes attributed to Carolan which he titled 'Carolan's Welcome'.

At first it was almost disturbing to play in such circumstances. The musicians realised that there was a crowd out there the like of which they had never witnessed in their lives. This caused them to wonder whether the PA system was able to cope with the situation. One thing of immediate concern was the eerie time lag between the end of each piece and the applause. Someone was able to assure them that the sound was fine, and the music going down well. And so it was. After the euphoria which greeted the Pope, they contributed to the music of the mass. It was a dramatic moment during the Offertory when the gifts were brought to the altar accompanied by the beat of the bodhrán bringing in the pipes and the other instruments. That day in the Phoenix Park there were over one and a quarter million people present, and it is estimated that the television viewing public amounted to countless millions around the world. In reliving the experience Paddy makes the claim that the Chieftains ought to be entered in the *Guinness Book of Records* as the folk group to have appeared before the largest audience ever, but adds with a modest grin, 'Of course it was, *basically*, the Pope's gig!'

Whether or not they ever make it into the *Book of Records*, the

Paddy Moloney and family before the arrival of Pádraig

The Irish National Ballet performance of
The Playboy of the Western World

James Galways appears regularly with the band.

In the elegant Royal Hospital, Kilmainham, Dublin

Chieftains have already no shortage of tangible trophies in evidence of their achievements. While many of these come from overseas, there are also those bestowed by agencies within their own country. One in particular was the VATS Extra Special Merit Award, given to them in 1984 by the Variety Artists' Trust at a Gala function in Dublin's Olympia Theatre.

Also in 1984, the International Federation of the Phonographic Industry of Ireland presented them with a golden disc to mark album sales in excess of a quarter of a million in Ireland alone. It was the first award of its kind and was organised by Bob McGoráin. This occasion could hardly have been more public for the presentation was made by Gay Byrne in the course of a *Late Late Show,* Ireland and the world's longest-running television chat programme. A note of hilarity was introduced when Gay produced Paddy's original ukelele, unearthed by his team somewhere in the parental home in Donnycarney. Gallantly he attempted to favour the gathering with a rendition thereon, but with difficulty. The ravages of time had left the venerable instrument with but two surviving strings.

It is natural that the Chieftains should be as prominently featured by the home-based media as they are abroad. Their many appearances on RTE have included both studio shows and programmes made on location. Of the latter *The Chieftains in Thomond* has been aired by many channels outside Ireland. It was filmed at Knappogue Castle in County Clare with narration by Cyril Cusack. An RTE Radio series produced by Mary Corcoran dealt with the history and development of the band by way of a number of conversations between Paddy and Padraig Ó Raghaille. At the time of recording Paddy secretly wondered whether there might be an underlying macabre object to the exercise. 'I had the feeling that this material was all going to be stored away and used as my obituary, so it was something of a relief to hear it not only transmitted but repeated.'

From time to time television companies from outside Ireland have run the band to earth in their own home environment. A programme in the Channel 4 series, *How to be Celtic,* was a case in point. It was directed by Douglas Eadie, an old friend from his days in the Scottish Arts Council. The programme revolved around the music and the lives of the Chieftains, and in concentrating on the musical roots of the individual members brought them back to their ancestral stamping grounds.

Images of Ireland was an imaginative series which collectively and individually reflected their music through the work of six crafts-workers and artists. Made by Alan Tongue in the Belfast studios, it was eventually transmitted on the BBC national network and later by several European stations. Paddy was pleased that one of the artists involved was Edward Delaney because of his long association with Claddagh Records. He himself has sat for a number of

Sting, when the rock group Police played at Leixlip Castle near Dublin

well-known painters, including three portraits by Edward Maguire. This led to his experiencing the strange sensation of meeting himself unexpectedly on the wall of the National Gallery in Dublin during an opening. Sitting for George Campbell resulted in a long friendship as well as the gift of a death mask of Beethoven, bequeathed him by the artist.

Considering the vast amount of newsprint devoted to the Chieftains by journals in so many parts of the world, it is ironic that Paddy's most unfortunate experience with the press should have involved an Irish paper. It all arose from a lunch date at El Viño's in London with Garech a Brún and Gloria MacGowran, the widow of the actor Jack MacGowran. During the meal they got into conversation with a nearby diner who proudly announced that he had been appointed to the Grand Order of the Knights of St Patrick. Paddy's response was to whip out the whistle and work his way through a jig which happens to be called 'The Knights of St Patrick'. The music attracted favourable comment from the other clients including a certain Ms Xaviera Hollander, celebrated author of *The Happy Hooker*. The management however was quick to point out that they did not encourage musical performance on the premises. Paddy put away the whistle, everyone returned to their plates, and that was it. End of incident.

For some reason the *Evening Standard* reckoned that the affair was worth a paragraph, which in turn was lifted inaccurately by a London correspondent of a Dublin paper.

On returning to Ireland Paddy was quickly contacted by a friend, to tell him that his picture was in the paper that night together with a story suggesting that the musical director of the Chieftains had been *thrown out* of El Vino's of Fleet Street in the company of *The Happy Hooker*. Within minutes this was all confirmed with his own eyes. For a start there was a pressing need for immediate explanations, especially to the two Mrs Moloneys — wife and mother. Thereafter an angry telephone call to the offending newspaper, whose representative was ultimately relieved that the aggrieved party was prepared to settle for a verbal apology.

Family sensitivities were somewhat mollified the following day — as it happened Good Friday — when another paper ran a front-page picture of Paddy and Seán Potts playing at a special service in the Pro-Cathedral. To his relief the assembled clergy, including an auxiliary bishop, were highly amused by the whole story. However it was a fellow Dubliner who had the last word, on recognising him emerging from the church:

'Paddy you were quite bloody right. They had no bloody business to chuck you out for playing an ould tune.'

In 1978 Paddy was approached by Joan Denise Moriarty, director of the National Ballet Company. What she had in mind was a project of quite exceptional challenge. Her scheme was to

Paddy with Garech a Brún and Marianne Faithful

CLADDAGH RECORDS

GREG HELGESON

choreograph a ballet version of *The Playboy of the Western World* to the music of the Chieftains, with the proviso that the group should play live for the dancers during every performance. The idea was agreed in principle, and subsequently Brendan Smith, director of the Dublin Theatre Festival, requested that such a production be performed in the Olympia Theatre during that year's Festival.

The dancers initially worked to a two and a quarter hours tape taken from the first seven Chieftains' albums, although when they eventually rehearsed with the group physically present they found this indeed added pep to the step. For the Chieftains it was a new, exhausting, but unforgettable experience. Some of the chosen

*Paddy and Burgess Meredith
at Venice, California in 1986*

pieces had been rarely played or almost forgotten, yet it was essential that not a beat or a bar be altered.

They operated by means of detailed notes on both the links and the various pieces included, but in practice there was no complete score in the usual sense. This is something which caused some admiration and wonder, especially among classically-trained musicians. Such techniques are applied in some Far Eastern formal dance traditions, but were virtually unknown to Western theatre at that time.

Prior to the opening night there were no more than three complete rehearsals involving the full company, yet the week-long run was a triumph with every performance a sell-out. After the Festival, which had been attended by the President and the Taoiseach, the ballet was performed in Cork, home of the National Ballet Company, where RTE televised the show. Later it ran for a successful fortnight on Broadway, and six years after its premiere was revived again in the Olympia. On that occasion Carolyn Swift of the *Irish Times* remarked that, 'It had lost nothing of its vivacity and charm.' Within days it went on to make a major contribution to the 1984 Belfast Arts Festival. The following year, according to accounts in the local press, two open-air performances of the ballet constituted the highlight of the Rennes Festival.

Paddy's major regret despite all the acclaim which has surrounded *Playboy* is that in the initial stages time did not permit him to compose a totally new score. This must remain an ambition unfulfilled; however the whole experience clearly showed to the public that the Chieftains were well able to cope with challenges of considerable complexity. There are of course ambitions still to be fulfilled. For Paddy perhaps the most far-reaching is to see the eventual founding of a National Folk Orchestra. Time will tell. But

The Colman Dance Ensemble from the USA at the Olympia Theatre, Dublin, 1986

this particular hope was expressed in his entry in the Irish *Who's Who* as long as a decade and a half ago.

Despite the many moments of high profile, generally in Ireland the Chieftains could in no way be accused of constantly courting the limelight. Each one finds the periods not committed to touring as essential time to devote to family, friends, or even pursuing individual musical interests. Six extremely individualistic personalities have adapted themselves to maintain a working relationship in the heightened atmosphere that goes with constant travel. There are of course moments of mutual irritation, but there is also a well of mutual respect. And when not on the road, a scattering of the ways is essential to keep the machine running smoothly.

Paddy has special difficulties in separating the professional and domestic sides of life due simply to his being musical director and on-going impressario to the group. Rita is prepared to accept that the daily routine is liable to be punctuated by a stream of phone calls, but understandably resents those who fail to accept that even professional musicians and their families have a right to some privacy. A quiet night at home is a luxury. As parents they have done their utmost to try and raise their children in a normal family atmosphere, although as she puts it, 'This can be difficult when you are walking down the street and someone runs up to the father to ask him for his autograph.' Not that any artist is ever unwilling to part with an autograph!

Even outside their private lives, many of the Chieftains' collective commitments at home are pursued away from the obvious glare of publicity. For instance two or three times a year they make a point of supporting the School of Irish Studies, placing them in the unusual position of playing to groups of largely American mature students but on Irish soil. After a long association, their contribution could be described as a regular part of the school curriculum. At the same time they also really enjoy these sessions, due in part to their being able to play without any form of amplification.

Another organisation which Paddy is always glad to support is Na Píobairí Uilleann, of which he was an original member. This is a unique association in that membership is restricted to active pipers. It was founded by Breándan Breathnach who was one of those he used to meet back in the days when prominent pipers came together in Peter Flynn's house. From time to time Paddy has performed for the association at musical evenings held at its Henrietta Street headquarters in Dublin, and has also attended its annual gathering in Bettystown, County Meath. In recent times he has also made a point of taking part in and bringing fellow musicians to sessions run by the Roundwood branch of Comhaltas Ceoltóirí Éireann organised to coincide with his returns from abroad. Roundwood is close to his home in County Wicklow.

Paddy with Jackson Browne at Lisdoonvarna, 1982

The late Willie Clancy was another regular at Flynn's and most of the present Chieftains try to make it to Milltown Malbay for the July summer school which commemorates him. Former Chieftains also tend to turn up, with Seán Potts one of the regular tutors. The school has grown to be an international event and yet its original warm spirit has survived the growth. A friendly atmosphere prevails throughout the week in which young learner musicians feel totally uninhibited in discussing their difficulties and their aspirations with some of the best-known traditional players in the world. Paddy considers this the best of all festivals.

Of course in Ireland, like everywhere else, major concerts are of considerable importance in maintaining the image of the band. One venue which has featured prominently in the engagement book in more recent years is Dublin's National Concert Hall. The Chieftains actually performed the first public concert in the hall after its official opening in September 1981. The following year this was also the scene for one of the most remarkable performances ever staged, when the band teamed up with the Tianjin ensemble of Chinese musicians, dancers, and singers.

Before the show Paddy had been intrigued to discover that the visiting instrumentalists utilised a system of notation identical to the tonic solfa which has been his constant aid since childhood. (In practice the Chinese express the system numerically, something which Paddy has since mastered in order to score for Chinese musicians.) This presented an opportunity too good to miss, resulting in the Chieftains and the Tianjin musicians coming together on stage to play the old Irish melody 'An Gaoth Aneas'. The audience was clearly moved to witness this unique fusion of two cultures. It was also prophetic of exciting things to come.

In 1984 the Chieftains came of age and once again the National Concert Hall provided the scene for the celebrations. It was a magnificent night, a gala concert in aid of the Irish blind olympic chess team. But more than that. Also a chance for the Irish public to share joyfully in the sense of achievement: twenty-one years of continuous music-making.

The line up included Chieftains past and present as well as Eamonn Kelly, the *seanchaí* of long associations with many of the musicians. It was, to put it mildly, a lively night with troupes of dancers and even the drum corps and a piper from the Rathcoole Pipe Band. The audience responded in a way which left no doubt as to its involvement in the sense of occasion. They loved every minute of it, and even before they left their seats a massive cake was wheeled on stage to the sound of popping corks. The Chieftains were well and truly at home.

Given the musical atmosphere in which he was reared, it is not really surprising that Matt Molloy should have been playing the flute like an expert by the age of eight. He grew up in Ballaghaderreen, a market town with broad streets in County Roscommon, servicing an agricultural community of small farms extending into parts of Sligo, Leitrim, and Mayo.

Ballaghaderreen lies in the heartland of an area which spawned the rich North Connacht instrumental style, famous for fiddlers and fluters alike. Many of the most famous of these emigrated to America in the earlier part of this century, but even from that distance they were still to prove a great influence on traditional music in Ireland

COLM HENRY

◄ *The group at the Self-
Aid concert, Royal
Dublin Society, 1986*

as the new wonder of 78 records started to filter back across the Atlantic.

By the age of eighteen Matt had picked up just about every possible national award to be won on his instrument. Around that time he came to seek employment in Dublin, and there he has lived for much of his life along with his wife Geraldine and four children. Before turning to music as a full-time career he worked as an engineer in Dublin airport. But music was always an essential ingredient to life, and that included a great deal of public performance. Soon after coming to the city he forged links with fellow traditional instrumentalists such as the Kildare piper Liam O'Flynn, the Donegal-born fiddler Tommy Peoples, and a certain Dubliner by the name of Paddy Moloney with whom he played three nights a week in the Old Shieling in Raheny.

When Matt became a Chieftain in September 1979 he was no stranger to group work, for he had already been an original member of the Bothy Band and later joined Planxty, two groups that contributed enormously and brought great class to the popular tradition in Ireland. He was the perfect choice to replace Mick Tubridy, for not only was he acknowledged as one of Ireland's finest soloists but he had also had experience of the rough and tumble way of life of a touring musician.

One of the many highlights of his career was a much acclaimed television programme in which he joined James Galway to play their instruments and chat about their music. It was a fascinating experience to see together two great Irish flute players who followed such different traditions of music. Ciarán MacMathúna acted as 'referee', but perhaps that is the wrong term for it was obvious that each had great respect for the other, and indeed they ended up with a joint rendition of a hornpipe.

Matt has made three solo albums, and it is clear that his working life with the group has in no sense inhibited his abilities as a virtuoso soloist. Although musically an individualist, he none the less still identifies with the regional style in which he grew up. It is an exciting brand of music, highly punctuated and full of subtle ornamentation that comes and goes almost before the listener is aware of it.

114

13 Off the Great Wall

In 1980 when the Chieftains were taking part in the Sense of Ireland Festival, one of the boxes of the Royal Albert Hall was booked by a party of obvious Far Eastern origin. It consisted of a number of musicians together with some diplomats attached to the London embassy of the Peoples' Republic of China. Shortly afterwards they sent a letter to the Chieftains inviting them as guests to their country. This was the first step in a long process which eventually resulted in the members of the band, some accompanied by their wives, stepping out of an airliner onto Chinese soil on 23 April 1983.

As finally arranged, the trip took the form of a cultural exchange visit. There was financial contribution from both Chinese and Irish governments, but no money in the usual sense. Even so, it was the most rewarding and exciting tour ever experienced by the group.

It turned out to be a well-documented trip for along with the band, their publicist Charlie Comer and tour manager Mick O'Gorman, and the chairman of Claddagh there travelled a recording unit and a camera crew led by Alan Wright, Brian Masterson of Windmill Studios, and artist and photographer Pat Liddy. This extended party resulted only after complicated negotiations between the Chinese Embassy in Dublin and Paddy, who was also greatly assisted by the Irish Ambassador to China, John Campbell.

A poster advertising one of the Chinese concerts

For Paddy the whole experience was the realisation of a lifetime's dream. Thirty years before, his circle of acquaintances in Dublin included a girl called Ling Fung from whom he picked up Chinese melodies. This interest in the music was soon complemented by a passion for the cuisine. In that department particularly the trip broadened his experiences, sampling as he did over two hundred and forty dishes. In the total national cuisine, there are of course some five thousand delicacies to choose from.

From the word go the red carpet was rolled out with a warm welcome from their hosts of the Performing Artists' Agency along with the Irish Ambassador and his staff. They had hardly arrived when they found themselves guests of honour at a great banquet thrown by the chairman of the Cultural Committee.

Beijing, formerly Peking, was the point of arrival, and early the following morning the Chieftains were on their way to the Great Wall. It was more than a sight-seeing tour, for they brought along their instruments to play a brief but absolutely unique concert

SHANACHIE

A promotional picture for the Chinese tour

116

from the vantage point of one of the turrets. Their new-found Chinese friends told them that in all its thirteen hundred year history this was the first time such a happening had taken place on the wall.

In these circumstances it was fitting that Paddy had prepared an arrangement entitled 'Off the Great Wall'. The music attracted a friendly mob of well wishers and such was the multitude that it was miraculous that nobody went so far as to actually fall *off* the Great Wall. Returning to the coach through the crowd was almost impossible, especially for Derek clutching his harp in a posture of protective desperation. Shortly afterwards each and all were well able to do justice to a splendid lunch at the Ming Tomb.

The following morning the band had the opportunity of meeting the Chinese musicians who were to join them in concert. Paddy made it his business to familiarise himself immediately with the basic principles of their various instruments, in order to get working on the musical arrangements for the planned combined performance. He found the instrumentalists intelligent and adaptable, as he had with the Tianjin ensemble previously in Dublin. Having completed the work and rehearsed, they all went off to tour the Forbidden City and visit the Peking Opera. This he described as 'simply beautiful'.

On the third day the Chieftains gave their first concert in China at the Red Tower Theatre. Beforehand there was a certain amount of nervousness for no one knew quite what to expect. Someone had suggested that Chinese audiences were different from those in the West; that they tended to discuss the music during performance, and that a lack of applause did not necessarily imply a lack of appreciation. It didn't turn out that way at all. The attention was undivided and the applause heart-warming. A Beijing newspaper, which described the Chieftains as 'the greatest exponents of traditional Irish music', went on to report: 'Eight Chinese musicians of the Chinese Broadcasting Art Group joined the Chieftains in presenting "The Wind from the South", "Planxty Irwin", and a Chinese tune called "Full of Joy". The performance evoked an enthusiastic ovation from the audience. Traditional Chinese instruments such as the Erhu and the Yangqin were blended with the Irish instruments in great harmony.'

A second concert, again attended by a capacity crowd of around a thousand, was equally warmly received. As on the former evening, a Chinese interpreter dressed in spectacular costume translated prepared notes on the music for the benefit of the audience. What rather impressed Paddy was the fact that the dearest seat in the house sold for about twenty-five pence.

On their final day in the capital the band visited the world-famous Beijing Conservatory of Music. Here they performed and were themselves entertained to a selection of pieces played by the Conservatory musicians. That evening there was a reception at the

Matt meets with a fellow flautist in China.

117

The first folk group ever to play on the Great Wall of China

In concert at Shanghai

Some Chinese fans outside a Shanghai theatre

Paddy tests a Chinese flute at a musical instrument factory.

Irish Embassy, with some of the party moving on afterwards to sample the delights of Mongolian cooking.

Suzhou, known as the Heavenly City and famous for its pure water and beautiful complexions, lived up to all expectations. An exquisite place of historic architecture where the trees meet each other above the centre of the streets and where bicycles are numbered in their tens of thousands. A city famous for its silk and for its instrument factory, where Paddy added to his own collection by purchasing a Cheng, a mouth-blown organ. Kevin took the opportunity to buy local percussion instruments and Matt acquired some Chinese flutes.

Although here the people were less familiar with visiting foreign musicians, the concerts were again exciting and memorable. The local instrumentalists at first seemed apprehensive at the thought of playing with the visitors, but in the event proved equally expert and adaptable as those in Beijing.

Perhaps the most unusual experience was that of visiting an agricultural commune near to Lake Taihu. Paddy had made a point of requesting to meet local non-professional musicians, and these turned out to be farm workers. Of all things, a session developed. The room where this took place was hardly able to contain the crowd of onlookers, from the very old to tiny babies. The house itself was a sort of ever-expanding witness to the locally revered concept of the extended family. The marriage of each member of the rising generation had been marked by the construction of another room.

From Suzhou the party travelled to Shanghai on a train journey which was in itself a high point of the tour. Here too the concerts were booked out, with the local musicians adding much to the magic of the occasion. The Irish were once again received in the Conservatory, and were intrigued to find evidence of individual regional musical style as had once pertained in Ireland. The Shanghai audience included Paddy Healy, a Kerryman working as a teacher in China. When the band struck up the polkas it was all too much for him. Grabbing Rita by the hand, he started dancing there and then in the auditorium. It was only fortunate that there wasn't a dreadful accident as the people in the balcony surged forward to get a look at what was going on down below.

Culinary adventures in this huge industrial city took in a remarkable vegetarian meal served in a Bhuddist monastery with the visitors working their way through twenty-three dishes. Elsewhere the band accompanied a session on a river-boat in which the Irish instructed their hosts as to how to dance a half-set. Unquestionably the river Yangtze had never seen the like before.

It was The Walls of Limerick which ended the final banquet, that and the director of the Cultural Bureau singing a haunting traditional song which put everyone in mind of the traditions of Connemara. It was a happy if nostalgic occasion punctuated by

Street musicians in Hong Kong

many a salutation of 'Gambei', a phrase which may be quite accurately translated as 'bottoms up'. No one was quite in control of the emotions the following morning when the Chieftains said goodbye to their hosts and interpreters and departed for Hong Kong.

The tour resulted in a film and an album, both entitled *The Chieftains in China*. The latter was issued by Claddagh early in 1985 (also by Shanachie in the United States), and faithfully reproduces much of the music as well as the atmosphere surrounding one of the most extraordinary adventures ever experienced by an Irish folk group. In addition to the Chieftains the disc, which quickly appeared in the charts after release, introduced the Chinese musicians as well as the interpreters describing the music to audiences. It was a difficult task to edit fourteen hours of tape down to about forty minutes, but on the sleeve — a beautiful gate-fold format containing pictures of the musicians on tour — there is a message in Chinese which sums up the real meaning of the tour. This translates into English:

'With their virtuosity, the Chieftains have successfully introduced traditional Irish music to the Chinese audience and won their hearts. These musicians are distinguished envoys of culture who have brought China and Ireland, both endowed with ancient cultural traditions, closer to each other.'

It is signed by Lin Lin, Vice-President of the Chinese Peoples' Association for Friendship with Foreign Countries.

Paddy is greeted by the Chinese minister for culture in Beijing

14 Black Wax – Putting It On Record

It would be impossible to plot the story of the Chieftains without considering the special relationship between the group and Claddagh Records. The Chieftains first came together for Claddagh to record what was then the company's second album, and in all the years since the association has been maintained. From time to time there have been numerous arrangements with a variety of recording concerns to facilitate international distribution, but for all that Claddagh has remained the mother company.

For Paddy this connection has been particularly pertinent due to his years as manager and later managing director of the company. When he accepted Garech a Brún's invitation to join, it entailed resigning a good steady job; however he had known Garech for many years, admired the idealistic basis on which he had founded Claddagh, and believed that he had a role to play in expanding its potential.

It was to prove a mutually beneficial arrangement. From his previous employment Paddy was able to bring with him experience in the commercial world as well as his knowledge of traditional music. At the same time, day to day involvement in the management of the company was to provide him with an invaluable knowledge of all aspects of the recording industry. Much of the actual *graft* was of an administrative and legal nature such as getting familiar with contract law, copyright, and the intricacies of publication, for Claddagh had the support of its sister music-publishing company, Woodtown.

Prior to that much, although not all, of his relationship with Garech had been of a more social nature. He had been a frequent guest at the famous series of parties in the fifties to which musicians and poets were summoned from far and wide. These were held in an old cottage on Garech's County Wicklow demesne with the food — potatoes, vegetables and suckling pig — served on huge platters on the floor and consumed without recourse to cutlery. Once a well-known fiddler, Tom Mulligan, a man of tremendous proportion, inadvertently placed a huge foot bang in the middle of the dish of spuds and skidded the length of the kitchen, only to arise unscathed.

Paddy has often paid tribute to the role of Garech a Brún as chairman of the firm, a much more active role than that of simply providing financial backing: 'He insisted on getting everything absolutely right, even to the point of delaying production.' This perfectionist streak was often expressed in the area of art work. From the commencement of its operations Claddagh specialised in high-quality sleeves, utilising the talents of artists such as Edward Delaney, Louis Le Brocquy, Edward Maguire, Catherine Folâtre, John Bellamy, Barry Cooke, Patrick Scott and the late Seán Kenny. Top photographers too, such as Jeffrey Craig, Claud Virgin, Angus Forbes, David Steen, Pat Liddy, Roy Esmonde, and John Morris were also engaged to maintain high graphical standards.

For Paddy one advantage in joining Claddagh was the opportunity of introducing Ioan Allen to the company, who for a period became a director, being himself a legend in the world of 'sound' and closely associated with Ray Dolby. Although Paddy's previous experiences were in the musical field, he none the less found himself engrossed in the techniques relating to recording the significant 'spoken arts' section of the catalogue. Poets and writers made an equal impression as the musicians with whom he worked and included Seamus Heaney, John Montague, Thomas Kinsella, Richard Murphy, Robert Lowell, John Berriman, and Samuel Beckett.

Paddy in 1984

It was a particular pleasure to play his part in focusing greater recognition on so many worthy traditional musicians and singers. Before joining the staff he had been involved in arranging and accompanying Dolly MacMahon's solo album, and later in the production field he was able to help bring artists such as Paddy Taylor, Máire Áine Ní Dhonnachadha, Seán Mac Donncha, Denis Murphy and Julia Clifford, Sarah and Rita Keane, and Tommy Potts before a wider public.

Tommy had been a boyhood musical hero and the particular demands in recording a great artist whose fiddle was virtually an extension of his personality were well rewarded by the quality of the album which eventually appeared. Tommy tended to work himself into any given piece, nor indeed was he beyond passing verbal comment as he played his instrument. All of this was indicative of his remarkably inventive spirit, however it did create some problems for Paddy and Ioan when it came to trying to isolate tracks with defined tops and tails.

From time to time Paddy, in conjunction with Garech a Brún, organised concerts in the Peacock Theatre to promote the recording artists — singers, musicians, and poets. He remembers Sarah and Rita Keane arriving in Dublin from Cahirlistrane, County Galway, to take part in such an event and bringing with them a brace of chickens as a present for Garech. It is a fond memory, for his grandmother used to do exactly the same when she came up to visit her family in the city. The record featuring the Keane sisters has long been regarded as a classic by aficionados of traditional singing. For Paddy, 'It was like listening to a double chanter when they sang.'

Seán Keane

Of all the records which he supervised, produced, or co-produced he has a particular regard for *The Star above the Garter* presenting the fiddles of Denis Murphy and Julia Clifford. He worked on this along with Gene Martin and although the tracks were taped in Dublin, initial preparation was carried out in Gneeveaguila in County Kerry. This inevitably resulted in nights abandoned to vigorous music and boisterous dancing in and around the heartland of the Sliabh Luachra tradition.

The Drones and the Chanters was something of a historic album as it featured no less than seven of the finest pipers in the land. Seamus Ennis, Peadar Broe, Dan Dowd, Tommy Reck, Willie Clancy, and indeed Paddy himself assembled in the same studio at the same time — something of a logistical miracle. Because of his stature in the pipering tradition, the album also featured Leo Rowsome post-humously, and it is sad to note that only three of these seven musicians have survived the intervening years since the recording was made.

Seán Keane's solo album, *Gusty's Frolics,* was recorded at the London studios of Angus McKenzie. McKenzie is known in the business as a brilliant 'sound man' who invariably produces marvellous technical work despite the handicap of being blind. His studio was also selected to engineer the *Tin Whistles* record featuring Paddy and Seán Potts. It was a measure of the informality of working conditions in those days that the pro-gramme for this LP was only finalised in the back seat of Barbara Dickson's car. It was the Scottish singer who gave the two whistlers a lift to their taping session in London.

No assignment was to prove more demanding than recording Ó Riada's orchestral work 'Hercules Dux Ferrariae', the major item on his *Vertical Man* LP. This took place in London and entailed hiring the Philharmonic Orchestra, with the composer himself insisting that Carlo Franci of La Scala be the sole conductor to whom he would entrust the interpretation of his score. After the work was completed there was an enormous sense of relief in the studio. There was also an hour of booked recording time still to run and Ó Riada's way of winding down was to organise a spontaneous jam session with himself, Paddy, and the entire string section of the orchestra. Somewhere the results of all of this have been preserved on tape.

Quite a proportion of the Claddagh catalogue has of course been devoted to the music of the Chieftains. Although a number of singles have been issued from time to time and proved important in terms of the charts, in general the record buying public would associate the group with albums. Those LPs (usually described numerically) which were released in fairly regular sequence proved vital to the development of the group as a recording band, a natural complement to its commitment to live performance. Reference has already been made to the influence of the first five albums in the more formative years (see *On the Road*) but this impetus has been maintained in more recent times. Each succeeding album has in itself been a milestone in the development and direction of the Chieftains.

Chieftains 6 or *Bonaparte's Retreat*, issued in 1976, introduced the fourteen-minute long musical montage by Paddy which gave the album its title. In a sense this was a logical follow-up to the previously recorded 'Battle of Aughrim', and confirmed that the public was open to the concept of the extended suite. It also further established the Chieftains as being prepared to step outside the usual recording format of most folk groups. In addition the record realised Paddy's ambition to have dancers batter the floor to the measure of traditional Kerry slides. Ten dancers are credited on the sleeve, although at the time it was rumoured that six were invited and thirty turned up.

The following year saw the issue of *Chieftains Live*, which was the first album to be based totally on concert performances recorded in fact at two venues, the Symphony Hall Boston and the Massey Hall Toronto. A similar approach was taken many years later with *The Chieftains in China* (issued in 1985). However in 1977 a second album was also released, *Chieftains 7*. This introduced a new element, as each member of the band contributed ideas for individual tracks through arrangement or composition. Paddy feels that this innovation in itself had some influence on the direction which their music was taking.

Chieftains 8 once again introduced the motif of the suite with the inclusion of the tone poem 'Sea Image'. Paddy had been nurturing this idea for many years, back indeed to the time when he cycled around County Clare with Mick Tubridy and had been struck by the richness of the sound of the sea at Lahinch. This music was also incorporated into the soundtrack of the film *The Grey Fox*, while coincidentally another item on the album 'An Speic Seoigheach' was featured in a film by Patrick Carey.

As well as these two pieces, there were a number of other tracks presenting the band at its best both ensemble and individually. Seán Keane evoked the spirit of the great travelling musician Johnny Doherty with the Donegal tune 'Seán sa Cheo'; Martin played a beautiful introduction to an unusual slow air version of the set dance 'The Job of Journeywork'; while Kevin provided his ever percussive pulse along with a blast of humorous gob music to lift a selection of polkas. Mick Tubridy raised his Clare roots on both flute and concertina, while Derek Bell also led on two different instruments in the harp piece 'Miss Hamilton'. Seán Potts was as usual splendidly everywhere, and on pipes Paddy never sounded better.

If anything the nineth album *Boil the Breakfast Early* surpassed its predecessor in critical acclaim. It featured an arrangement of the Carolan piece 'Mrs Judge' and no doubt classical commentators were aware that there had been in fact an earlier arrangement of this written by a certain Ludwig Van Beethoven. A dramatic item was the march from *Oscar and Malvina,* an eighteenth-century ballet based on the Ossianic legends, with the Chieftains joined by a corps of drummers. The final track was given over to a typical medley of reels, jigs, and slides called 'Chase around the Windmill'. This was a reminder that the album was made at Dublin's Windmill Studios. Paddy, who has personally produced all the Chieftains' discs, enthuses about the expertise and the facilities at Windmill, especially the talent of the senior engineer Brian Masterson and his extraordinary sensitivity for traditional instruments.

The tenth album was somewhat cosmopolitan in mood. As ever there was a wide selection of Irish pieces, but in addition tracks were also devoted to Manx and Breton music, a French Christmas carol, and the now familiar country-American 'Cotton Eyed Joe'. One track, 'Garech's Wedding', was the Moloney way of marking the marriage of his friend, the chairman of Claddagh, to Princess Purna Harshad Devi Jadeja.

To listen to all the Chieftains' albums, from the very first as recorded in Peter Hunt Studios to the recent collaboration with James Galway (and not forgetting the examples recorded in the company of orchestras) is akin to assimilating a living history of the group. In fact putting the music on wax has amounted to creating a tangible history. It will all be there for future generations to judge for themselves, long after the roar of the crowds in so many concert halls around the world has passed beyond the realms of living memory.

15 *New Directions*

Paddy Moloney is one of the few musicians to have remained close to his traditional background and yet also investigate the challenge of new musical directions. Although the public has only learnt of this aspect of the man since the Chieftains started to attract widespread attention, the urge to innovate has always been turning in the system since first he started to play music. At fourteen years of age for instance, doodling on the piano somehow or other worked itself into a little composition solemnly entitled 'The Ivy Waltz' — the presence of an ivy bush conspicuously outside the window was not entirely unconnected.

This drive to arrange, compose, and improvise, which was reflected in his musical work at school, began to develop very consciously through his early involvements with ceili bands, the trio, and the quartets. The process continued through his association with Ceoltóirí Cualann to blossom eventually with the founding of the Chieftains. By the time *Chieftains 2* was released the approach was well established in pieces such as 'The Fox Chase', or

The finale of the Self-Aid concert, Dublin 1986. The Edge from U2 is to Paddy's left.

later 'The Trip to Sligo' on the third album. Be that as it may, the discerning ear on hearing the very first album should be able to detect the intricacies of cross-rhythms and the teasing out of counter melodies. In other words, arrangement and composition were an accepted part of the package from the day when the Chieftains first came together.

By the time *The Battle of Aughrim* was recorded there could be no doubt that the band and its musical director were not only traditional in approach but also innovators in spirit. This was clear enough from the very sound of the music, although few realised that Paddy had spent hours simply imbibing the atmosphere of the original battleground in County Galway before attempting to write down so much as a note of music. The finished product was to find favour in a variety of musical circles. Dr Gerard Victory, then musical director of Radio Telefís Éireann and one of Ireland's most noted contemporary composers, sought Paddy's approval prior to scoring an orchestral interpretation but one essentially based on the original work. In the early seventies, at one concert the Chieftains actually joined forces with the RTE Orchestra for a special performance in the Carlton Cinema.

One might cite the ballet music for *Playboy* as a prime and successful example of this urge to explore new musical forms. In a sense it was, but not essentially in the area of composition and arrangement. In this instance the new challenge was really one of performance. The band was required to function according to a very different and exacting discipline, and did so with distinction.

Although he has always been interested in broadening his musical horizons, Paddy himself reckons, 'I only really got my teeth into composition with *Tristan and Isolde.*' The score for the film was recorded in 1979, although there had previously been a number of successful ventures in the area of programme music. In 1975 *Barry Lyndon* was the first major feature film made for the cinema to which the Chieftains contributed, winning them an Oscar. Two years later the group recorded the music for *The Purple Taxi,* directed by Yves Boisset. On this occasion the group was augmented by a seventy-piece string section. In early 1978 Paddy found himself working on the first of two films entitled *Ballad of the Irish Horse,* this one funded by Bord na gCapall. The National Geographic Society film of the same name came much later, in 1984, with the bulk of the arrangement and composition being written in Cape Cod during an alleged Summer vacation at the home of his friend Jack Davitt.

Paddy's original plan for *Tristan and Isolde* was to score the music for himself on pipes together with a chamber orchestra. As he got more involved in the job he became convinced that the character of the work called for the additional participation of the full group. Even the orchestra increased in dimension as the score developed: the chamber ensemble originally catered for eventually grew to a

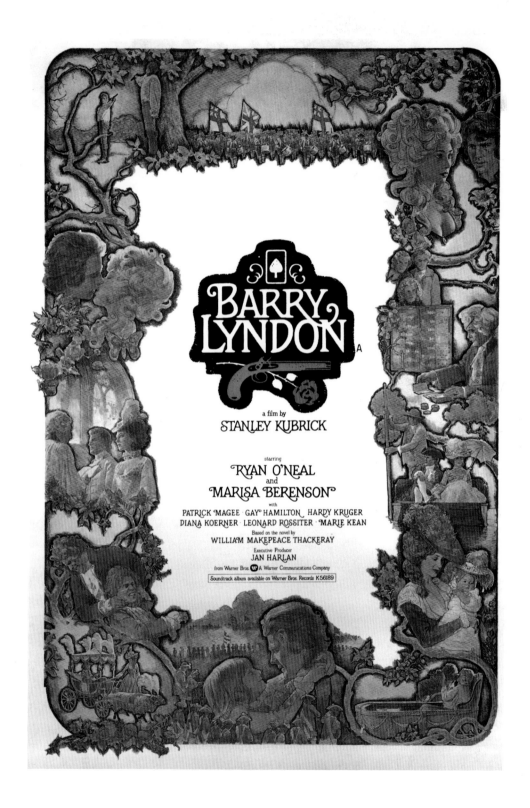

COLM HENRY

Paddy demonstrates the uilleann pipes to Mike Oldfield.

COLM HENRY

132

full symphony outfit. This music probably represents the first attempt in an extended original work to incorporate the uilleann pipes in an orchestral setting.

The challenge composing this work was at the time awesome because of its sheer size. From the early stages he was at least confident of being on the right track when he witnessed the director, Claire Labine, shed tears of appreciation on first hearing his initial musical ideas. The film, which was shot in Ireland, had a strong cast including Richard Burton, Kate Mulgrew, Nicholas Clay, Cyril Cusack, Geraldine Fitzgerald and Niall Toibín. The only pity was that various considerations precluded it being

generally released, although this misfortune did not render the work on the music a waste of time. Quite the opposite: the finished score has been frequently performed and proved a major boost to Moloney's reputation as a composer of programme music. It has been played by orchestras such as the Irish Chamber, the Ulster, and the Milwaukee and Toronto Symphony Orchestras. In July 1985, the Toronto performance attracted a capacity audience of around eight thousand. Two of the pieces, the love theme and 'The March of the King of Cornwall', are included in the album made with James Galway.

Another important assignment was writing the music for Philip Borsos' *The Grey Fox*, which starred Richard Farnsworth. Although the director approached this film with tremendous enthusiasm, he was surprised at its eventual commercial success. It went on to win seven awards in Canada and caused the Chieftains to share the 1983 Genie citation for 'best music'. A year later there was further acclamation in Hollywood in the form of a Grammy nomination. It should be noted that the score included an original composition by Martin Fay.

Yet a further major commission was the score for *The Year of the French,* the television adaption of Thomas Flanagan's novel which was made by RTE in conjunction with ORTF of France and Channel 4. It was logical that this should eventually be issued as an album, and after some negotiation it was agreed that there would be an independent recording for LP purposes which brought together the Chieftains and the RTE Concert Orchestra conducted by Proinnsías Ó Duinn. Earlier during the filming of the series the Chieftains had themselves appeared in one of the excerpts, thinly disguised in costumes of the late eighteenth century.

Paddy strongly argues the case for arranging separate recording sessions should a programme score be issued eventually as an album. When engaged in writing for film he is always conscious of the necessity of submitting to the restraints demanded by the all-important visual aspects. In practice this may mean having to give up the development of an interesting musical idea because of the action on screen. However freed from the discipline of the sound-

Kevin and Paddy prior to taking the stage at Dublin's Self-Aid concert, 1986

track, there is no reason why such ideas should not be expanded in the version of the score designed for a record. This is why he tends to be less than enthusiastic at the notion of LPs being taken directly from sound-tracks.

How in fact does an instrumentalist with a background in traditional music cope with the techniques of scoring for film? Moloney was of course educated in the broad aspects of musical theory, but finds the most convenient way of approaching a score (including all instrumental parts) is through tonic solfa. When he reaches the final stages in the sequence of composition he works in

134

close cooperation with Derek Bell who is highly skilled in converting the material into notated parts for the various sections.

As well as this obvious ability, Paddy acknowledges his friend's flair in suggesting fresh ideas to enrich the colour of the overall work, especially in the sphere of harmony. 'He is very good to work with, has great understanding, and we get on very well. Indeed quite simply he's a musical genius.' This admiration would appear to be mutual, judging from the contents of a paper which Bell wrote on the subject of Moloney's compositions. He argued that these deserved a recognised place in the total corpus of Irish music — a recognition which he suggested should take the form of an honorary degree from an Irish university.

The lengthy business of composing film music starts with the director giving Paddy a copy of the script. Having read this he begins searching for some basic musical themes. 'I walk around the place like an *eejit* looking for inspiration', sometimes conscious of the neighbours viewing this stage of the creative process with some astonishment. Inspiration can strike at the most inconvenient times such as when behind the wheel of a car, in which case the only thing to do is to pull over and jot down the idea before it is lost forever.

Composition for the artist who is not only often on the road but also frequently in the air poses special problems. There are numerous historical examples of unusual manuscripts which have been used to capture the embryo of creative works, from the bark of trees to the walls of caves. The chances are that Moloney has uniquely added to the list in the form of airflight *vomit* containers. 'When flying during tours I often reach for the sick bag and write down all sorts of things that come into my mind about the music.' During a trip he sometimes collects as many as twenty or thirty such documents, covered in scribbles.

Irrespective of the medium for memorising his ideas, from the word go he thinks in terms of defined musical phrases. His basic rule for composing for film in particular is that each separate cut should add up to a logically constructed melodic unit, with a beginning, middle, and end. In *Tristan and Isolde* there were fifty-two such cuts which gives some idea of the work involved. Finding the tunes is the first priority, and only after this is achieved does he move on to tackle the problems of arrangement and choosing his instrumental options.

Frequent consultation with the director gives Paddy the assurance that his end of the project is progressing in line with the overall shape of the film, although the detailed work of finely timing the music is one of the last tasks, not undertaken until the viewing of the rushes. After that a certain amount of adjustment to the score may be required, although in practice there tends to be a reasonable spirit of give and take between director and composer. However, the piper recognises that ultimately it is the director who calls the tune. This in itself is a good reason to argue for an

Handing on the tradition to young Pádraig Moloney

PÁDRAIG O FLANNABHRA

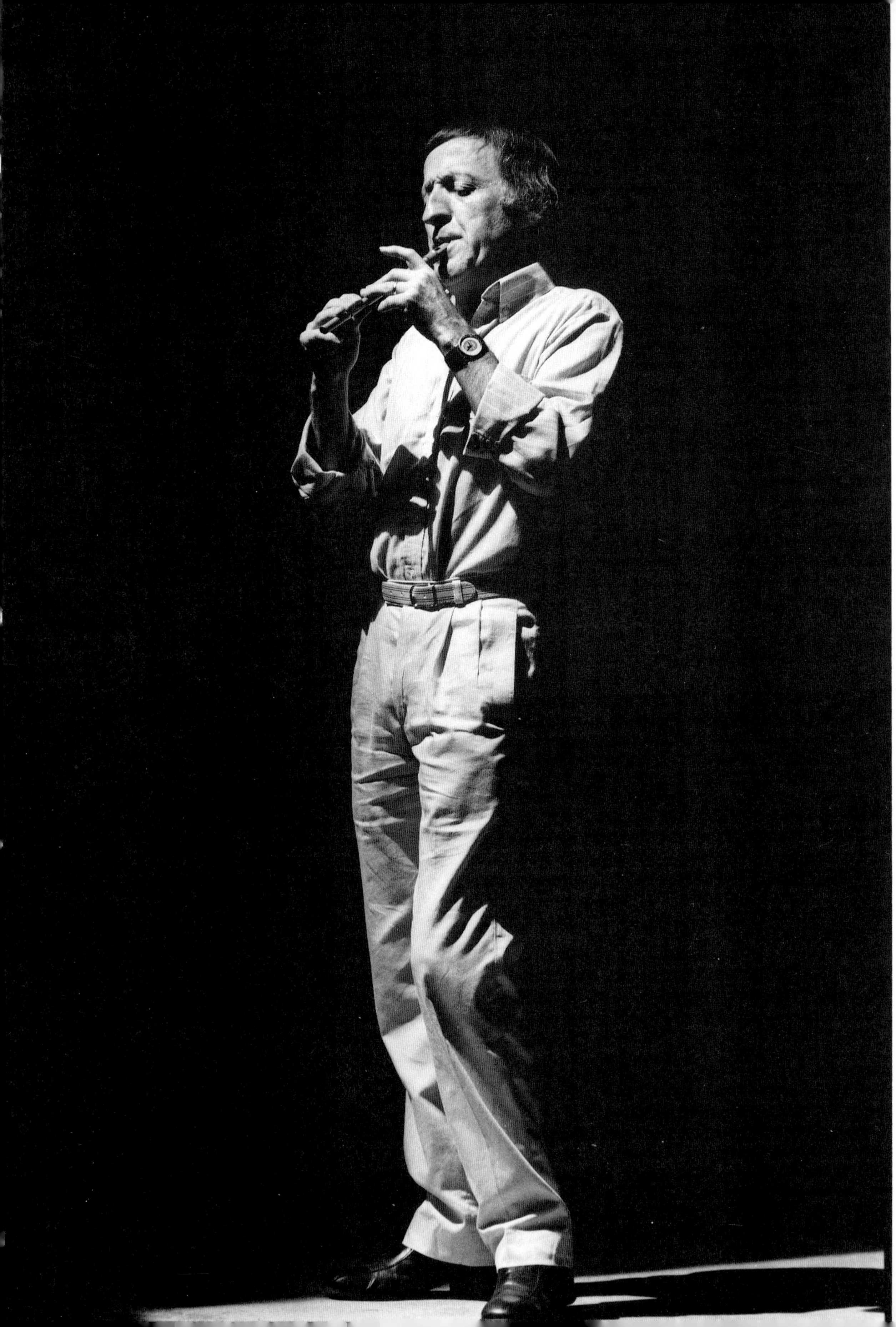

NANCY ELLISON

J. T. MILLER

expanded version of the score should a commercial recording of the music be proposed.

How important to Paddy is this commitment to composition, and especially the composition of film music? Unquestionably, as he says himself, 'It is very exciting and very interesting.' It is also engrossing and fatiguing. When the process is underway there are times when total solitude is absolutely necessary, often swiftly followed by equally essential periods of intense involvement with others.

In the future this aspect of his working life is likely to assume increasing importance. There are many new musical ideas turning over in his mind and waiting for the right moment to take shape. Yet it is typical of Moloney that he is reluctant to comment on such things until he feels that the time is ripe, and only then after consultation with his colleagues. 'I take great delight in this type of work, but public performance is still our main thing.' By that, which puts it in a nutshell, he means continuing to play traditional music before live audiences in the company of the Chieftains. This has always been the top priority and will remain so for many years to come.

16 Discography

Albums featuring The Chieftains

Claddagh CC2   The Chieftains   1963
Side 1
1. Sé Fáth mo Bhuartha, The Lark on the Strand, An Falaingín Muimhneach, Trim the Velvet
2. An Comhra Donn, Murphy's Hornpipe
3. Cailín na Gruaige Doinne
4. Comb your Hair and Curl it, The Boys of Ballisodare
5. The Musical Priest, The Queen of May
Side 2
1. The Walls of Liscarroll
2. An Druimfhionn Dhonn Dílis
3. The Connemara Stocking, The Limestone Rock, Dan Breen's
4. Casadh an tSúgáin
5. The Boy in the Gap
6. St Mary's, Church St Polkas, Garrett Barry's, The Battering Ram, Kitty goes a-milking, Rakish Paddy

Claddagh CC7   The Chieftains 2   1969
Side 1
1. Banish Misfortune, Gillian's Apples
2. Planxty George Brabazon
3. Bean an Fhir Rua
4. Pis Fhliuch (O'Farrells Welcome to Limerick)
5. An Páistín Fionn, Mrs Crotty's Reel, The Mountain Top
6. The Foxhunt
Side 2
1. An Mhaighdean Mhara, Tie the Bonnet, O'Rourke's Reel
2. Callaghan's Hornpipe, Byrne's Hornpipe
3. Pigtown, Tie the Ribbons, The Bag of Potatoes
4. The Humours of Whiskey, Hardiman the Fiddler
5. Donall Óg
6. Brian Boru's March
7. Sweeney's, Denis Murphy's, The Scartaglen Polka

Claddagh CC10   The Chieftains 3   1971
Side 1
1. Strike the Gay Harp, Lord Mayo, The Lady on the Island, The Sailor on the Rock

2. Sonny's Mazurka, Tommy Hunt's Jig
3. Eibhlí Gheal Ciúin Ní Chearbhaill, Delahunty's Hornpipe
4. The Hunter's Purse
5. The March of the King of Laois
6. Carolan's Concerto
Side 2
1. Tom Billy's Reel, The Road to Lisdoonvarna, The Merry Sisters
2. An Gaoth Aneas
3. Lord Inchiquin
4. The Trip to Sligo
5. An Raibh Tú ag an gCarraig?
6. John Kelly's Slide, Merrily Kiss the Quaker, Denis Murphy's Slide

Claddagh CC14   The Chieftains 4   1974
Side 1
1. Drowsey Maggie
2. Morgan Magan
3. The Tip of the Whistle
4. The Bucks of Oranmore
5. The Battle of Aughrim
Side 2
1. The Morning Dew
2. Carrickfergus
3. Hewlett
4. Cherish the Ladies
5. Lord Mayo
6. Mná na hÉireann
7. O'Keeffe's Slide, An Suisín Bán, The Star Above the Garter, The Weavers

Claddagh CC 16   The Chieftains 5   1975
Side 1
1. The Timpán Reel
2. Tabhair Dom do Lámh
3. Three Kerry Polkas
4. Ceol Bhriotánach (Breton Music)
5. The Chieftains Knock at the Door
Side 2
1. The Robber's Glen
2. An Ghé agus an Grá Geal (The Goose and Bright Love)
3. The Humours of Carolan
4. Samhradh, Samhradh
5. Kerry Slides

Claddagh CC20   Bonaparte's Retreat   1976
Side 1
1. The Chattering Magpie
2. An Chéad Mháirt den Fhomhar (The First Tuesday of Autumn), Green Grow the Rushes
3. Bonaparte's Retreat
Side 2
1. Away with Ye
2. Caledonia
3. Iníon Nic Diarmada (or the Princess Royal), Máire Dhall (Blind Mary), John Drury
4. The Rights of Man
5. Round the House and Mind the Dresser

Claddagh CC24   The Chieftains 7   1977
Side 1
1. Away we go again
2. Dochas
3. Hedigan's Fancy
4. John O'Connor, The Ode to Whiskey
5. Friel's Kitchen

Side 2
1. No. 6 The Coombe
2. O'Sullivan's March
3. The Ace and Deuce of Pipering
4. The Fairies' Lamentation and Dance
5. Oh! The Breeches full of Stitches

Claddagh CC21   The Chieftains Live   1977
Side 1
1. The Morning Dew
2. George Brabazon
3. Kerry Slides
4. Carrickfergus
5. Carolan's Concerto
6. The Foxhunt
Side 2
1. Round the House and Mind the Dresser
2. Solos: Cáitlin Triall, For the Sakes of Old Decency, Carolan's Farewell to Music, Banish Misfortune, The Tarbolton/The Pinch of Snuff, The Star of Munster/The Flogging Reel
3. Limerick's Lamentation
4. O'Neill's March
5. Ríl Mór

Claddagh CC29   The Chieftains 8   1978
Side 1
1. The Session
2. Doctor John Hart
3. Seán sa Cheo
4. An tSean Bhean Bhocht, The Fairies' Hornpipe
5. Sea Image
Side 2
1. If I had Maggie in the Wood
2. An Speic Seoigheach

3. The Dogs among the Bushes
4. Miss Hamilton
5. The Job of Journeywork
6. The Wind that shakes the Barley, The Reel with the Beryle

Claddagh CC30 Boil the Breakfast Early   1979
Side 1
1. Boil the Breakfast Early
2. Mrs Judge
3. March from Oscar and Malvina
4. When a Man's in Love
5. Bealach an Doirnin
Side 2
1. Ag taisteal na Blárnán
2. Carolan's Welcome
3. Up against the Buachalawns
4. Gol na Mban san Ár
5. Chase around the Windmill

Claddagh CC33   The Chieftains 10   1981
Side 1
1. The Christmas Reel
2. Salut à la Compagnie
3. Kiss me Kate
4. The Custom Gap, The Spindle Shank, My love is in America
5. Manx Music
6. Master Crowley's Reels
7. The Pride of Pimlico
Side 2
1. An Faire
2. An Durzhunel
3. Sir Arthur Shaen, Madam Cole
4. Garech's Wedding
5. Cotton Eyed Joe

Claddagh CC36   The Year of the French 1982

With the Radio Telefís Éireann Concert Orchestra
Side 1
1. Killala: The Main Theme
2. The French March
3. The McCarthy Theme
4. Treacy's Barnyard Dance
5. The Irish March: March of the Mayomen, Uilleann Pipes Lament
6. Killala: The Main Theme
Side 2
1. The Irish March: March of the Mayomen
2. Cunla, The Yearling Fair Reel
3. Killala: The Opening Theme, Killala: The Coach Ride
4. The Bolero: McCarthy's Arrest
5. The McCarthy Theme, The Wandering
6. The French March, Cooper's Tune
7. The Hanging, Sean Ó Dí
8. Killala: The Main Theme

Claddagh CC42   The Chieftains in China   1985

Side 1
1. Full of Joy
2. In a Suzhow Garden
3. If I had Maggie in the Wood
4. The Reason for my Sorrow
5. The Chieftains in China

Side 2
1. Planxty Irwin
2. Off the Great Wall
3. A Tribute to O'Carolan
4. The Wind from the South
5. China to Hong Kong

Claddagh CCF15   Ballad of the Irish Horse 1986

Side 1
1. Ballad of the Irish Horse: Main Theme
2. Going to the Fair (Hornpipe)
3. The Birth of the Foals
4. Galway Races
5. Lady Hemphill
6. Horses of Ireland: Part 1

Side 2
1. Chasing the Fox
2. The Green Pastures (Jig)
3. Sceal na gCapall: The Story of the Horse
4. The Boyne Hunt, Mullingar Races, The Five Mile Chase (Reels)
5. Horses of Ireland: Part 2

Warner Brothers K56189   Barry Lyndon   1976
Music from the film including tracks by The Chieftains

In preparation

James Galway and The Chieftains
Breton music by The Chieftains
Self-Aid album

CBS JC34975 Watermark
Art Garfunkel with The Chieftains

Some of the above Claddagh discs were also released on other labels.

A selection of albums featuring The Chieftains as individuals or in various combinations

Gael Linn CEF010 Reacaireacht an Riadaigh
Seán Ó Ríada and Ceoltóirí Cualann, including Paddy
Moloney, Martin Fay, Seán Keane, Michael Tubridy, Peadar Mercier, and Seán Potts

Gael Linn CEF012   The Playboy of the Western World
As above

Gael Linn CEF027   Ó Ríada sa Gaiety
As above

Gael Linn CEF032   Ó Ríada
As above

Claddagh CC15   Tin Whistles   1975
Featuring Paddy Moloney and Seán Potts

Claddagh CC11   The Drones and the Chanters
Including solo tracks by Paddy Moloney

Virgin Records VIL12043   Ommadawn   1975
Featuring Mike Oldfield with contribution by Paddy Moloney

Virgin Records V2222   Five Miles Out   1982
Featuring Mike Oldfield with contribution by Paddy Moloney

CBS S26395   Milladorio, Solfafria
Featuring Paddy Moloney

Asylum Records 52365   I Can't Stand Still
Featuring Don Henley. Including track *Lá Eile* by Paddy Moloney and Derek Bell

Claddagh CC27   The Eagle's Whistle   1979
Featuring Michael Tubridy

Comhaltas Ceoltóirí Éireann CL5   The Castle Ceili Band   1973
Including Seán Keane and Michael Tubridy

Claddagh CC17   Gusty's Frolicks
Featuring Seán Keane

Ogham Records BLB5005   Seán Keane   1981
As above

Claddagh CC18   Carolan's Receipt
Featuring Derek Bell

Claddagh CC28   Carolan's Favourite   1980
Featuring Derek Bell and The Chieftains with the New Ireland Chamber Orchestra conducted by John Beckett

Claddagh CSM51   Derek Bell Plays With Himself   1981
Featuring Derek Bell

Claddagh CC35   Derek Bell's Musical Ireland
As above   1983

Ogham Records BLB5008   From Sinding to Swing 1984
As above

Trailer LER 3035   Prosperous   1978
plus Tara 1001, Tara 2008
Christy Moore *et alia* including Kevin Conneff

Mulligan LUN004   Matt Molloy   1976
Featuring Matt Molloy
Polydor 2904018   The Heathery Breeze   1981
As above

Mulligan LUN017   Matt Molloy, Paul Brady and Tommy Peoples   1978

Mulligan LUN002   The Bothy Band
Featuring the Bothy Band including Matt Molloy

Mulligan LUN007   Old Hay You Have Killed Me
As above

Mulligan LUN015   Out of the Wind Into the Sun
As above   1977

Mulligan LUN030   After Hours   1979
As above

Mulligan LUN041   The Best of the Bothy Band
As above   1981

Green Linnet SIF1058   Contentment is Wealth
1985
Featuring Matt Molloy and Seán Keane with Arty McGlynn

Single

EMI R6054   Paul McCartney, Ebony and Ivory
Side B Rainclouds, featuring Paddy Moloney